HOW TWO CALIFORNIA SURFERS TURNED THEIR LOVE
OF THE OCEAN INTO AN AMERICAN SUCCESS STORY

FITS LIKE A
GLOVE

The **Bill & Bob Meistrell** Story

Adam
Do What You Love
Love What You Do
Bill M...

FRANK GROMLING

OCEAN PUBLISHING

ISBN 978-0-9826940-6-0

Ocean Publishing
200 S. Oceanshore Boulevard
Flagler Beach, Florida 32136
(386) 517-1600
www.oceanpubishing.org

Book cover, layout and design by Nate Myers, Wilhelm Design

Editing by Linda Ellis, The Editing Place

Photo Credits:

Photographs by Body Glove International were taken by Mark Kawakami, Mike Balzer, or Brent Bielman.

Photographs from the Meistrell Archive were taken by various Meistrell family members or were given to the family for use as it wishes.

All other photographs are by those individuals identified with their photographs throughout the book. Printed in the United States of America

Front Cover: Surfing image from Body Glove. Diving image from PhotoXpress.com

10 9 8 7 6 5 4 3 2 1

CONTENTS

PREFACE

This is the story of how two poor farm boys from Missouri ended up surfing and diving in California and building a successful international business while having the time of their lives.

As kids, we had three specific goals: to be treasure hunters, to own a submarine, and to be deep-sea divers. At that time, in rural Missouri, these goals all seemed so far out of reach. Now, sixty years later, I smile as I look back and realize that we accomplished all of them. But I'm more happy about the bigger accomplishments, those things we have done for others.

Body Glove has impacted so many by opening up the adventure of the ocean to millions of people throughout the United States and around the world. We never would have dreamed of that, but now it is a reality.

And, along the way, Bill and I learned one important lesson: Go for your dreams. The water is fine. Jump in unafraid with both feet. Life is to be experienced and enjoyed.

Bob Meistrell
Redondo Beach, California
May 2013

FOREWORD

Alex Gray in Tahiti at the legendary Teahupoo. This wave was a pivotal moment in his young career and helped get him an invitation to the Eddie Aikau Big Wave Surf Contest.
Photo credit: Ben Thouard

Foreword: Alex Gray

can't remember the last time I surfed without a Body Glove wetsuit. As I was growing up in the South Bay as a beach baby, my parents always had me in day-glow Body Glove wetsuits. Body Glove is synonymous with the South Bay beach culture and lifestyle.

At eleven years old I was honored with my first sponsorship from Body Glove. After I met Bill and Bob Meistrell, I was addicted to the company and the people who ran it. Family-owned businesses are rare and hard to find these days. Especially one that has thrived for sixty years.

As a team rider for Body Glove over the past sixteen years, I have had the pleasure of growing up with the company. What always strikes me the most is how involved Bill and Bob were. Unfortunately, they are no longer with us. But their spirit lives. Until he passed, Bob remained one of the best influences of my life. He treated all the people he met as if he had known them for their entire lives. His greetings were always accompanied by a warm smile and friendly hug. Bob would usually ask if I had any girlfriends in my life, then tell me they must be blind if they were hanging out with me (laugh). My favorite part of seeing Bob was his incredible stories. I love Body Glove, so listening to Bob's stories was like having a life-size, animated book on tape. I typically found myself picking my jaw up off the floor after hearing stories about shooting through Hermosa Pier during the '50s on a wooden surfboard, or diving hundreds of feet deep to scavenge an old shipwreck. There is nothing the Meistrell brothers haven't done in the ocean.

They were the backbone of our surf industry. But the way Body Glove truly separates itself is by its core values. I don't consider myself a sponsored athlete by Body Glove. Through their uncanny amount of love and support, I consider myself part of the family. And this feeling is an extension of the Meistrell brothers' morals and beliefs. I would like to thank the Meistrell brothers and Body Glove for everything they have done for our beloved surf community and me. I consider myself a Body Glove team rider for life, and look forward to the company's next sixty amazing years.

Alex Gray, South Bay, California

Peter (PT) Townend always surfed with style.
Photo credit: Mike Moir

Foreword: Peter "PT" Townend

grew up in the tropics of Coolangatta, Australia, and never really thought about wearing wetsuits for the first surfing years of my life until I went to Bells Beach for the Australian Titles in 1971. And, for a Queenslander, it was friggin' cold.

Steve Core introduced me to Fred Pyke, who represented Dive N' Surf in Australia. Fred hooked me up with suits and became my first sponsor, thereby beginning my relationship with the Meistrell family, which has lasted through more than forty years of professional surfing to this day.

The impact that Body Glove had on the development of pro surfing in America cannot be underestimated. Starting in the early '80s, Body Glove's Winter Grand Prix and Bud Surf Tour launched the professional careers of Kelly Slater, Shane Dorian, Shane Beschen, Rob Machado, Pat O'Connell, Jeff Booth, Dino Andino, and countless others.

The Meistrells are one of the great surfing families, like the Keaulanas, Hoffmans, O'Neills, Alters, Youngs, Paskowitzs, Downings, Currens, Webers, Nolls, and others who were instrumental in making our surf culture what it is today. This book shares some of the adventure, contributions, and fun the Meistrell family has had over the past sixty years.

Peter (PT) Townend, Huntington Beach, California

DEDICATION

To my twin brother, Bill. My mirror, business partner, and eternal best friend.

And to the love of my life and soul mate, Patty.

Bob Meistrell
May 2013

On behalf of my four children, Kenna, Robert, Rhoni, and Randi, I want to thank my dad and my uncle Bill for all the fabulous times they shared with us. They left behind a great legacy, and now it has become our responsibility to keep the "dream" alive. Along the way, there were many "wipeouts," but the "tube rides" are what we will remember always.

Robbie Meistrell

To my dad and my uncle Bob, who were able to accomplish so much, build a successful company out of passion, and create a surfing and diving lifestyle that so many people strive to live today. My dad and my uncle Bob, along with my mom, Jackie, and my aunt Patty, taught us to love what we do and do what we love.

Bill Meistrell Jr.

INTRODUCTION

Body Glove International: 1953–2013

Dive N' Surf and Body Glove International began in 1953 when twin brothers Bill and Bob Meistrell, two young surfers just back from military service in the Korean War, bought into a recently opened diving and surfing shop aptly named Dive N' Surf. The name "Body Glove" came about years later when Bill Meistrell said the new neoprene wetsuits he and Bob were making "fit like a glove."

This year the company celebrates its sixtieth year in business as a privately held, family owned and operated American business. Although Bill passed away in 2006, Bob remained the company's active spokesperson until his sudden death in June 2013; now, two younger generations of Meistrells lead the company. Over the past sixty years, Body Glove transformed itself from a small retail dive and surf shop in Redondo Beach, California, into a multimillion-dollar international marketing giant. Its unique

Body Glove logo, once found only on wetsuits, now is on every kind of water sports equipment, gear, and clothing.

This is the true story of the Meistrell brothers' contribution to the development of the wetsuit, the Southern California beach culture, and Body Glove International.

Bill and Bob Meistrell moved to California from rural Boonville, Missouri, when their mother relocated the family to Manhattan Beach in search of employment and a better life. It was 1944, and the boys were just sixteen years old.

While they first made wetsuits in Redondo Beach, Body Glove now manufactures cutting-edge, quality, attractive products throughout the world and offers them at a fair price to make life in the water and at the beach safe and enjoyable. Body Glove is represented on every continent except Antarctica. Its standards of quality and performance remain as high today as they were in 1953.

It is this history of innovation and love of the ocean that challenges Body Glove to make products fitting the lifestyle of every water sports enthusiast. Body Glove is proud to be one of the last family owned dive and surf businesses, and pledges to continually build products that enhance and protect enthusiasts both above and below the water's surface.

The Meistrell family is happy to say that many of its friends and partners have been with them for the long haul. They also are proud of the amazing friendships and partnerships forged over sixty years of business. Body Glove treats its friends and employees as family, and many have been part of that family for multiple decades. The company truly values its relationships with its loyal customers, current and former athletes, trade groups, photographers, retailers, suppliers, media partners, nonprofit organizations, celebrities, and the other amazing brands in the water sports and action sports community who inspire owners and employees on a daily basis.

Through the twins' fascinating lives, unveiled in the following chapters, Bill and Bob's passion for water sports and adventure continually drove them to create new and better products for waters sports everywhere, all the while following their personal mantra of "Do what you love, love what you do!"

BORN IN
THE USA

One night in July, 1928, identical twins Bill and Bob Meistrell came into the world. Their births signaled the beginning of a life of challenge and adventure for two boys who would grow up to revolutionize the worlds of surfing and diving, and greatly influence the beach lifestyle.

In one of those quirks of life, Bill and Bob Meistrell were born twenty minutes apart—Bill just before midnight, on July 30, and Bob just after, on July 31.

Bob (left) and Bill were inseparable from the beginning.
Photo credit: Meistrell Archive

The boys' father was killed by his former business partner when they were not yet four years old. With their two brothers and three sisters, the twins and their mother worked hard to make it through the tough economic times of the Great Depression.

After their father's death, their mother, Mary Elizabeth, moved the family to a farm outside of town. And, to the boys' great surprise, there was a pond behind the house. Bill and Bob discovered they loved water, any kind of water, and the pond and a nearby swimming pool quickly became targets of their growing obsession to explore under

1

their surfaces. The brothers had three goals: to own a submarine, to go deep-sea diving, and to find lost treasure. In their lifetime together, they would accomplish all three, but for now their adventure focused squarely on something less exotic—a five-gallon vegetable-oil can.

What fourteen-year-old Bill and Bob were up to was the creation of their first diving helmet. As Bob described it, "We got a five-gallon vegetable can, cut out the bottom, and soldered tin shoulder pads on it so it didn't cut into us. We put a piece of glass on the front and used tar as a seal around the glass."

As hard as it may be to conceive, the boys broke off chunks of tar from the road, and chewed it until their saliva made it soft and pliable. They stuck the chewed-up tar around the glass faceplate to seal it. Amazingly, it worked. Mostly. They remembered the tar tasting terrible and leaving a mess in their mouths.

Knowing they needed to be weighted to stay underwater, they used lead ingots from their grandfather's mercantile store, most of which ended up on the bottom of their pond.

Bill and Bob as Boy Scouts in Boonville, Missouri.
Photo credit: Meistrell Archive

All the parts used in Bill and Bob's first attempt to explore underwater.
Photo credit: Meistrell Archive

With a tire pump and a garden hose inserted into the can, they ventured into the pond. From reading about diving, Bill and Bob knew enough to put in a check valve, of sorts, made from a marble and a spring, to stop the air from rushing out when the brother above water stopped pumping. Every once in a while, the pump would get so hot they had to put it in the water to cool off. As Bob remembered,

> You would see the helmet start to fill with water when the person on top was dipping it in the water. Then all of a sudden you would hear the pumping start up again and the water started to drain out.

> We started in a nearby municipal pool and then ventured to our own lakes. The first place we dove with it was in Kemper Military Academy lake. We would march out into the middle of the lake, and all you would see was a hose sticking down and bubbles coming up.

They wore shoes so they wouldn't hurt their feet stepping on twigs and other debris on the bottom.

If they leaned over, water would flow into the helmet, so they didn't lean over, and they didn't see very much. No one else was doing what they were doing at the time. In the lake there were a lot of perch and snapping turtles. Bob recalled, "When we were walking around, we would stir up the turtles. They were over a foot long and they could break a stick with their bite." Or a toe or finger.

Bob continued, "One of us would wear this thing in the swimming pool, sit down on the bottom and read magazines, while the other pumped air on the surface with a tire pump. I can't tell you how many times we had to bail out of that thing. It's a wonder we didn't get an air embolism."

> *Air Embolism: The presence in the tissues and blood of a gas, such as air or nitrogen bubbles, caused by an injection of air or, in the case of nitrogen, by an abrupt and substantial reduction in the ambient pressure.*

Bill and Bob growing up in Boonville, Missouri.
Photo credit: Meistrell Archive

Growing up in rural Boonville, Missouri, the youngest two of the family, Bill and Bob found all kinds of adventures. As twins, they always had their "best friend" with them to share spoken and unspoken feelings, thoughts, and ideas. Often, one would start a sentence and the other would finish it. They quickly discovered that being twins was a special opportunity, one they would cherish all their lives.

Bill and Bob fishing on their handmade boat.
Photo credit: Meistrell Archive

In the picture above, Bill and Bob are fishing on a lake in a boat they made from scrap wood. Knowing Bill and Bob's love for the water, their mother dammed the seven streams that ran through their property to make a lake for them.

On the farm they had so many jobs they could hardly keep track of them. When they were just nine or ten, they hauled drinking water to the workers threshing and baling in the fields. Although small for their age, they even helped load the bales onto wagons and trucks.

Their older brother Joe started to grow tobacco. In fact, he was one of the first to do so in Missouri. The boys were hired by Joe to pick tobacco worms, big green things that ate the leaves, and earned a penny for every ten worms they captured and killed by sealing into jars.

Their mom told them that if they could catch a pig, they could have it. So they figured out how to lasso a sow, which pulled them all over the yard. When it finally tired, they wrestled her to the ground and tied her legs as they'd seen cowboys do in the movies.

Bob figured he would raise pigs, especially since he heard they had lots of babies, which meant lots of potential money. Even though sheep had only one or two lambs each year, Bill decided that he'd raise them rather than pigs. According to Bob's telling of the story, his sow ate all of her piglets and he never earned a dime, while Bill did pretty well selling sheep.

Bill Meistrell's son, Billy, has a favorite story about his uncle Bob, the one about the time Bob got hired by a neighbor to stack firewood. Billy believes the story shows a part of the early formation of Bob's ethics and business sense.

It was a winter day in Missouri. Bill didn't go to school because he was sick. It was so cold that the teachers let the students out early that day. Bob decided to walk home a different way, and on his walk he saw an old man stacking firewood. Bob told him that he'd stack the wood for him, and the man didn't believe he could do it. The man asked how much Bob would charge, and Bob said he would accept anything the man thought the job was worth. Bob ran home to tell his mom that he had gotten a job and would be gone for about three hours.

Bob worked until sundown. He put the big pieces, medium pieces, and small pieces into three different piles. At the end of the job, Bob knocked on the door and the man came out to look at the pile of wood. He said what a good job Bob had done and that he hadn't thought Bob would be able to do it. The man asked how much he owed, and Bob said, "I will be happy with whatever you give me." The man handed Bob a nickel, and Bob took it, thanked him, and started walking away. The man stopped Bob and asked if he was satisfied. Bob said, "I am satisfied, because that was our agreement; however, I will never work for you again." His mother had taught him to say thank you, even if he wasn't happy. She taught him to accept what he was given and walk away.

As Bob walked down the stairs from the man's front porch, the man said, "Son, come back up here." Reaching into his pocket, the man pulled out a $5 bill and handed it to Bob.

For the balance of Bob's time in Missouri, he worked for the man by cleaning his house, shoveling snow, and doing odd jobs. Mary Elizabeth Meistrell's ethics teaching would last a lifetime for the twins.

At their grandfather's mercantile store, the boys worked stocking shelves and cleaning up. While they didn't get paid in cash, they earned rewards from their grandfather who gave them small treats from time to time. The most valuable reward was learning how to be successful in a retail store by treating customers right. Little did they know that these lessons would stick with them for their lifetime and prove to be invaluable in building a successful business.

Bill and Bob cleaned a public swimming pool three times a week by scrubbing the sides with brushes. In return, they got to swim there all they wanted. This job enabled them to do what they loved more than anything—being in the water.

They helped a milkman deliver milk to homes throughout town, and they set bowling pins at the local lanes. Bob even worked for a short time as a butcher, until he nearly cut off his thumb and decided to find another, safer, job. The boys dragged a wagon around town to collect metal, which they sold for cash that they put into their savings account. As her way of teaching them financial responsibility, their mother added matching amounts to their deposits, and the boys could see the balance increasing nicely. This was amazing, considering that at the time the country was going through the Great Depression.

Neither Bill nor Bob remembered much about their father. After all, they were only four when he was killed. What they recall vividly, and with much passion, are the many family times in Missouri, all revolving around one strong person—their mother, Mary Elizabeth.

If the boys did something wrong, she took a switch to their bottoms. According to Bob, their mother could give a strong talking to them that was so bad they dreaded the talking to more than they dreaded the switch.

According to Bill and Bob's sisters, their mother never cried, at least in public. They remember her as an extremely strong woman. After their father died, she managed the family business and tried to collect money that people owed them. Some people paid her, but most didn't.

Bill and Bob's father, John Leo Meistrell, was born on September 15, 1889, in Boonville, Missouri, the tenth and youngest child of Nicholas and Margaret Meistrell. He married Mary Elizabeth Fischer on April 23, 1913, and they had seven children, Bill and Bob being the youngest.

John Meistrell was known in Boonville as an astute, fair, and honest businessman who made solid investments in land and people. He often loaned money at reasonable terms to townspeople needing help during the difficult years of the 1920s.

While visiting Boonville years later, Bob met a local businessman who told him a story about his dad. The man said he himself had been a juvenile delinquent years before and still owed a lot of people money. "I asked your dad for money to start a business. Your dad gave me $500 and said, 'Do you know why you are going to pay me back?' and I said, 'No, why?' Your dad said, 'Because I am the only person in town that is going to loan you money.'" And the man paid him back.

John's business partner during most of that time was William Kingsbury. On the night of April 7, 1932, however, the partnership came to a sudden and shocking end. As reconstructed by Boonville police, after an argument between the partners several weeks earlier, Kingsbury apparently shot and killed John in his office. He then locked John's body inside the firm's vault.

Because John did not return home, and Kingsbury had disappeared, police initially suspected a double kidnapping until the next day when Kingsbury's lifeless body was found at a cemetery in St. Louis. Kingsbury apparently shot himself in the head with the revolver that was found on the ground near his body. After receiving a report that Kingsbury had been seen leaving the company's building the night before, the police searched John's office and found his hat on the floor. The police ordered the vault opened, and they found John lying inside with two gunshots to his body and one to the head.

Bill and Bob, not quite four years old, were fatherless. Mary Elizabeth, mother of seven, was faced with the daunting challenge of burying her husband and caring for a large family of seven children, all under the age of fourteen. While she had always been a loving wife and mother, her faith, strength, and intelligence quickly became evident to all as she was forced to refocus her life after John's death.

Three days before he was killed, their dad had loaned a man in town $5,000. Their mother went to the man and asked if she could have back some of the money to help pay expenses. Because it was a recent loan, she figured the man still had the money. He told her he had repaid the money to her husband the same day he borrowed it. Knowing her husband would have kept track of it, she asked if the man had paid with a check. The man said it was a pure cash deal.

Thirty years later, when Mary Elizabeth went back to Missouri for her mother's funeral, the same man, wanting to clear his conscience, found out she was in town and approached her. He said he had lied to her and now wanted to pay back the $5,000. She said, "I needed it then, I don't need it now."

In 1937, Mary Elizabeth married a man who had three children of his own. They worked together to build a new life and attempted to recover some of the money owed the Meistrells. Through their combined skills, they built a large fortune, which included seven farms and the successful mercantile store once owned by Mary Elizabeth's grandfather.

Soon, her husband took the twins on trips that often included having up to ten trucks following behind them. As he traveled throughout the Missouri countryside, he bought sheep at extremely low prices to be sold at auction for handsome profits.

At first, the boys' stepfather never drank alcohol. Bob remembered that many times at the hardware store he saw his stepfather being offered a drink, which he always refused. One day, as if a switch had been flipped, he took an offered drink and he soon became unable to resist temptation.

He began to make bad investments and in a couple of years they had lost everything. Mary divorced him and once again set about the arduous task of rebuilding her personal life and financial life.

About this same time, the boys' older brother Joe moved to Manhattan Beach, California, to work in the busy wartime aircraft industry. In 1944 their mother decided to relocate the family to the West Coast where, she had learned from Joe, the aircraft industry needed more workers and the pay was good. The family sold their now meager possessions, packed up the family car, and headed west in search of a new life. For Bill and Bob, with dreams of submarines, deep-sea diving, and lost treasure, this was bittersweet news. They loved the farm and its watery adventures, plus they had good friends in Boonville. California was some far-off place they had read about in books and magazines, maybe even at the bottom of a pool.

2

FROM FARM TO SOUTH BAY

In 1944, after siblings Joe, John, Judy, Mary Ann, and Fran had already moved to California, the remaining Meistrell family members— twins Bill and Bob, their mother, and their grandmother—drove to Manhattan Beach, where their Southern California adventure began in earnest.

Bill and Bob were in the tenth grade, so they enrolled at Redondo Beach Union High School in the mid-

The Manhattan Beach Pier in the early 1940s. Photo credit: Jan Dennis

dle of their sophomore year, in a class of two hundred students. Coming from Saints Peter and Paul, a small Catholic school in Missouri where there were only twenty kids in their class, this was a major shock for the young teens.

The transition from rural Missouri farm life to a growing California city wasn't easy for the twins. The kids in their classes made fun of them and, in one mean act, spray painted "Okies Go Home!" on their garage. While at first that hurt the boys, they laughed as they realized their supposedly superior classmates didn't even know the difference between Oklahoma and Missouri.

They wanted to join the swim team, but the school did not have a pool on campus and the Redondo Beach swim team did not have a great reputation. But the boys heard about somewhere that did. The nearby city of El Segundo had a public pool for its residents and, since their sister Judy lived in El Segundo, they figured they could use her address and swim all they wanted at the public pool. They got kicked out more times than they could remember.

At the start of their senior year, Bill and Bob transferred to El Segundo High, where they joined the swim and football teams. While Bill played halfback on the football team for the entire season, Bob's football experience was much different. He broke his back making a tackle on the first play of the first game. Carried off the field and taken to the hospital, Bob knew his football days were over. He was bedridden for six weeks. During that time he went through some intense depression. One day he decided to blindfold himself for twenty-four hours. When he finally took the blindfold off, he realized how fortunate he was and

Bob and Bill with their grandmother and mother when they moved to Southern California. Photo credit: Meistrell Archive

Bob (left) and Bill with their grandmother in 1946. Photo credit: Meistrell Archive

Bob (left) and Bill were pool lifeguards after they
moved to the South Bay.
Photo credit: Meistrell Archive

Looking south from the Manhattan Beach Pier in
the 1940s toward the sands of Hermosa Beach
and Redondo Beach.
Photo credit: Jan Dennis

Bob Meistrell with one of his original
surfboards.
Photo credit: Meistrell Archive

that he didn't have any problems. Fortunately, after five weeks of therapy, he recovered and resumed physical activities, especially swimming.

The El Segundo High School swim team was the best in the nation that year, being the only high school team to win first place in the Junior Nationals. Placing first in Juniors allowed them to compete in the Senior Nationals, where they placed second. After winning the Juniors, they were pitted against the San Diego Swim Club, Los Angeles Athletic Club, San Francisco Athletic Club, and the college teams from UCLA, Michigan State, and Ohio State, among others.

Even though the Pacific Ocean at Manhattan Beach was polluted at that time, both boys fell in love with the ocean and soon began surfing in the South Bay area of Manhattan, Hermosa, and Redondo beaches.

> In the '40s and '50s, raw sewage and street runoff drained directly into the ocean in the Manhattan Beach area and elsewhere along the coast. Also, natural seepage of oil from underneath the ocean floor produced copious amounts of tar that stuck to beaches and required turpentine and rags to clean from surfboards and feet.

Bob and Bill tried their hand at another diving-helmet adventure, this time with a genuine diver's helmet they picked up for just $25. When their mother asked why it cost so little to buy a barely used professional helmet, a double-piston air pump, 50 feet of hose, and shoe weights, the boys told her the truth: the previous owner had died wearing it because it didn't have a check valve.

One brother pumped air while the other walked around the Redondo breakwater at depths of 10 to 15 feet. After a few minutes underwater they'd surface with bloodshot eyes and occasional bleeding ears, testimony to their lack of knowledge about pressure. With wetsuits not yet invented, and the Pacific Ocean notoriously cold, they quickly became chilled but always stayed longer than was reasonable because it was so much fun to see the whole new underwater world before them.

At the same time Bill and Bob were exploring the world of underwater diving, they were becoming increasingly enamored with surfing. They took to surfing with the excitement they had shown for diving and every other sport. Bill and Bob hit the surf whenever possible with a variety of boards they took from their quiver for different surf conditions.

They began surfing at the Manhattan Beach Pier with a couple of lifeguards, plus the Kerwin brothers and several surfers, including Hap Jacobs, Bev Morgan, Dale Velzy, Bing Copeland, and Greg Noll, all of whom became famous names in the surfing world.

A very crowded Manhattan Beach on a nice summer day in the 1940s.
Photo credit: Jan Dennis

Bob and Bill loved to surf with their friends, as in this photo on the north side of the Manhattan Beach Pier.
Photo credit: Meistrell Archive

Cover of pamphlet produced by the city to attract visitors, with surfing one of the main attractions.
Photo credit: Jan Dennis

Greg Noll: "Well, to give you a little history on the Manhattan Beach Pier, Bobby and Billy were around from almost the first time I remember looking at the ocean. Those guys were inseparable. I started surfing in the Manhattan Beach Surf Club, and they were both members of the club. They were surfing all the time. You could hardly ever see one of them without seeing the other."

3

PROTECTING THE BEACHES

After graduation from high school, both Bill and Bob followed their love of the ocean and applied for jobs as lifeguards. They credit the Kerwin brothers of Hermosa Beach with convincing them to join the lifeguard service. The Kerwins, who became well-recognized names in the surfing community of South Bay, knew the Meistrells from their many days of surfing together around Hermosa and Manhattan Beach.

As Bill and Bob had been lifeguards at the pool back in Missouri, it was only natural for them to want to become beach lifeguards.

In the spring of 1947, Bill and Bob took the lifeguard qualification test, along with Walt Puffer, John Horne, and Bob Sheldon, who were also from El Segundo. Walt remembers the test as

Bill Meistrell in Manhattan Beach lifeguard chair in late 1940s.
Photo credit: Meistrell Archive

a grueling event of two heats of about sixty-five candidates. It started with a long swim of about 1,000 meters that started south of the Hermosa Pier and ended on the north side. Bob remembers swimmers all around him, kicking him in the face and pulling on him to upset his concentration and stroke. It was a fight for the job, and a lot of people wanted it.

Lifeguards on Tom Blake paddle boards monitored the swimmers to make sure everyone was safe. Only the top fifty swimmers were selected to continue the test, which was a "run-swim-run" contest, and all five El Segundo boys made the cut. The candidates then had to run 100 yards on the beach, swim out 200 yards, return, and run another 100 yards on the beach.

The last phase of the physical testing was called a "can-tow-line-swim"; each candidate had to swim out with a lifesaving can to a lifeguard who was acting as if he were drowning, and swim back to shore with the help of a lifeguard on the beach who pulled on a rope attached to the can.

If a candidate scored well on all of these tests, he progressed to an oral interview with a veteran lifeguard and a representative from the Los Angeles County civil service commission. Once the decision was made about how many lifeguards would be needed on the beach, final selections were made. Bill, Bob, Walt, John, and Bob Sheldon joined the ranks of the prestigious lifeguard corps protecting the local beaches. Bill and Bob were assigned to Hermosa Beach, Walt Puffer and John Horn went to Zuma Beach, and Bob Sheldon got El Porto.

While their first jobs came in the summer, when more guards were needed, they soon became full-time lifeguards and eventually worked all of the stations along the Los Angeles County coast.

By the time Bill and Bob joined the lifeguard corps, Los Angeles County had taken over several local lifeguard services and merged them into one organization. Although lifeguard services had existed along the coast for a number of years, getting their start in the 1920s and '30s, the centralization of the lifeguards under one county staff helped to create a more professional and capable organization.

Bill and Bob's lifeguard class.
First Row: Sabu, Greg Noll, Don Grannis, Joel Stallder, Bill Meistrell.
Second Row: Bob Meistrell, Buzzy James, Bev Morgan, Fred Zerkie, Jim Enright.
Photo credit: Meistrell Archive

Bob remembered performing 149 rescues in one year, most of which he called "preventative rescues," where he would extract someone from rip currents running from shore into deeper water.

One time in Redondo Beach, while working with another guard, he heard someone yelling for help at the breakwater. There wasn't much surf, and a small boat had just pulled onto the beach. Bob told the guy in the boat to take him out to the breakwater, where he found a boy trying to save a friend by holding his head above the water. The boy was tiring rapidly.

Bob saw that the victim was unconscious, so he bear-hugged him. The boy regained consciousness and vomited in Bob's face. But another life was saved.

It wasn't all work and no play for Bill and Bob and the other lifeguards. All of the lifeguards from that period remember the parties that sprang up after hours at different locations along the beach. Walt Puffer shared that "All the girls at the time thought the lifeguards were hot, so we had a good pick of dates. Lifeguards were all pretty good-looking guys, in shape and tan. The big social event of each summer was the Lifeguard Dance at the Biltmore Hotel in Hermosa Beach, two blocks from the pier. It had everything: dancing, drinking, fighting, and skinny-dipping."

The next two and a half years were fun for Bill and Bob as they surfed as often as they could, worked as lifeguards, and learned more about the ocean. They enjoyed life to the fullest—and then everything changed dramatically.

Bill (left) and Bob as Los Angeles Country Lifeguards. Photo credit: Meistrell Archive

Bob in the classic lifeguard attire: red shorts. Photo credit: Meistrell Archive

4

KOREA CALLS

As the United States entered the Korean War, Bill and Bob decided to join the Navy, but when they tried to enlist, Bob was rejected because of his high school back injury, and Bill wouldn't enlist without his brother. Shortly afterward, however, life on the beach ended abruptly for Bill and Bob when they were called into the Army. The Korean War was changing the lives of many young men in America, and Bill and Bob were drafted in 1950. Bob thought he wouldn't be accepted, but as he remembers it, "They said, 'You're warm, you're breathing, you're in.'" While Bob was assigned to the Army's Fort Ord induction center in Monterey, California, in an administrative role, Bill was shipped off to Korea. This was the first—and last—time the twins were ever separated, and neither of them liked it.

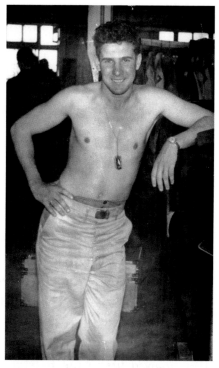

Bill on active duty.
Photo credit: Meistrell Archive

Bill's tour in Korea saw him assigned to a heavy mortar company on the front lines. He had thought he was signing on for a heavy "motor" unit, because he was interested in fixing and working on things. Despite his wish to avoid the front lines, ultimately Bill earned a Bronze Star for bravery.

Because Bill had worked for a telephone company before being drafted, he was sometimes given work repairing the unit's communications equipment. In Korea, communication between units was hardwired and run on the ground, and where Bill was stationed the lines had been severed somewhere in a valley between his unit and another. There were heavy artillery and counterattacks in the valley, and the US troops were taking heavy fire. Because the lines were down, the troops could not request help. Against orders, Bill went running from the camp with a large spool of wire to try to re-establish communication. He ran about a mile.

His unit's commander, Captain Baron, told two other guys to follow Bill, which they did for a little while, but when they saw all the enemy activity, they figured there was no way

Bill in combat fatigues.
Photo credit: Meistrell Archive

Bill in South Korea.
Photo credit: Meistrell Archive

Various images from Bill's time in Korea.
Photo credit: Meistrell Archive

Bill in Korea.
Photo credit: Meistrell Archive

he was alive. When they returned to camp, Captain Baron ordered them to look again. The men didn't find him the second time, either.

Before nightfall Bill walked into camp without a scratch after re-establishing the communication lines. Based on the significance of his brave act, he should have received the Silver Star, but because he was a communications technician and wasn't "allowed on the front lines," the army gave him the Bronze Star. Captain Baron said Bill was the bravest soldier he ever commanded.

Incredibly, even while in Korea Bill succeeded in finding time to get into some water. On a Rest & Recuperation break at a beach in Pusan, he found a guy sitting on a high chair, like those used by lifeguards back in the States. Bill asked him if they needed more lifeguards, and the guy told him to swim out to a black object offshore. Bill thought it was a lifeguard test, "So I beat the water to a froth, and when I got back, he told me I was a good swimmer." Then the guy asked Bill what the black

Billy Meistrell (left), Captain Baron and Bob at a reunion for the 40th Infantry.
Photo credit: Meistrell Archive

thing was. He and others had watched it for three days and thought it might be a shark. Bill told him it was a big rock, then turned in disgust, because the lifeguard obviously wasn't much of a lifeguard, and headed on down the beach.

While Bill was fighting for his country in Korea, Bob had drawn an easier assignment in Monterey, California, and quickly found places in Santa Cruz where he could surf. He and Patty, whom he married on November 8, 1950, lived in several different apartments and homes in Monterey, Pacific Grove, Seaside, and Santa Cruz in Bob's twenty-four months at Fort Ord. One day Bob and Patty took a trip north and stumbled on Santa Cruz. They instantly fell in love with the little town, and Bob liked the surf he saw there, too, so he and Patty decided to live there, even though it was forty-five miles from Fort Ord.

Bob hitchhiked to work until one day he met a man in a coffee shop who worked in the Army's photographic section, and after that Bob rode with him most mornings. One day after his shift, Bob got a ride from Captain Jefferson, an administrative officer at Fort Ord, and ended up riding home with him every night. Bob tried to pay for the gas but the captain wouldn't accept any money, so Bob did his yard work to repay him for driving him home.

While in Santa Cruz, Bob and Patty lived at Pleasure Point and at Seventeenth Street, both locations near the ocean. Not many people surfed the ocean in Santa Cruz at that time. Every time Bob took a trip back to the South Bay, he loaded up his car with the new "lighter" surfboards and sold them in Santa Cruz to surfers who were hungry for the innovation. He was more interested in having people to surf with than he was in the money he earned.

Bob surfing in Santa Cruz while stationed at Fort Ord.
Photo credit: Meistrell Archive

Bob often surfed after work during the week at Pleasure Point. While this was easy in the long summer daylight hours, surfing in the dark evenings of winter was more challenging. He'd park his car overlooking the ocean and turn the headlights on, directing them toward one large rock to give him some idea of the surf and how the waves were breaking. With luck, he'd get in about fifteen minutes of surfing before he got too cold to continue.

Every weekend when the surf was good, he'd call his friend Chuck Nichols, who lived twenty miles inland in

Los Gatos, to tell him to get down there right away. They wore wool sweaters that had a kind of oily texture to them. When the sweaters got wet, the guys would take them off, whip them around their heads to dry them as best they could and put them back on.

Another place Bob surfed in Santa Cruz was at the mouth of the San Lorenzo River where it flowed into the ocean. He, Patty, and their one-year old son Robbie cooked out on the shore of the river, and then Bob would paddle down the river and out to the ocean. There was never anyone else surfing there. But Bob did find one new friend on these frequent outings.

A little seal approached Bob several times, often staying very close. One time Bob brought anchovies with him and fed some to the seal, who climbed right up onto the front of his board. The seal balanced on the board as Bob surfed to shore.

Patty Meistrell in Santa Cruz while Bob was stationed at Fort Ord.
Photo credit: Meistrell Archive

Bill Bob 1952

Bill (left) and Bob when they returned home.
Photo credit: Meistrell Archive

It was in Santa Cruz that Bob realized more than ever that there had to be a way to reduce the potential for hypothermia from the cold Pacific Ocean and the cool northern California air. He realized that wearing woolen sweaters, and rushing to a campfire on the beach or to the heater in his car to get warm, was just not enough. Nothing worked well. He knew something had to be done, but a solution was years away.

The twins after honorable discharges from the U.S. Army in 1952.
Photo credit: Meistrell Archive

5

SURF'S UP, DIVERS DOWN

Bill returned from Korea in October 1952. His return to the United States was through Fort Ord, where Bob was still stationed, and he spent a week visiting with Bob. In his inimitable fashion, Bob thought he'd play tricks on his army buddies.

Posing as Bob, Bill was sent on various errands around the base. This might have worked out okay except for one difference. Because Bill had earned the combat infantry badge, he could blouse his boots, the military practice of tucking one's trousers into the tops of one's boots. Bob could not do that because he didn't have the combat badge, which was presented only to soldiers who had served in ground combat conditions.

When soldiers who had served with Bill in Korea came through Fort Ord and saw Bob, they always thought he was Bill and asked how he had returned home so quickly before them. When Bob told them "I was never there!" they didn't believe him, and Bob would finally give in and tell them he was Bill's twin. Even Bill's former unit commander, Captain Baron, mistook Bob for Bill when they met on the post.

After Bob's release from the military in December 1952, he and Bill returned to the South Bay and began a new phase in their lives—diving. Bill had bought an Aqua-Lung air tank, and Patty bought Bob one as a present. Without any instruction, long before professional diving courses had been developed, they dove locally and learned how to survive, making potentially deadly mistakes as they went along.

Another successful lobster dive off Palos Verdes.
Photo credit: Bev Morgan

Bob remembered well his first dive off Sapphire Beach. "I almost drowned because we didn't have quick-release weight belts. I was wearing a dry suit, the only kind of diving suit made at that time. My dry suit had a hole in the bottom, and it filled up with water. I had used an army cartridge belt as a weight belt, and I couldn't get out of that damn thing. The only thing that saved me was my 8-foot hand spear. I kept poking that spear into the bottom and pushing myself to shore, but Bill, my so-called safety man, wasn't paying any attention to me. The buddy system didn't exist in those early days." This incident is one example of many that helped Bob formulate some strong opinions about the buddy system and its importance.

The effects of the cold Pacific water and the cool Southern California weather troubled Bill and Bob, as they did all California surfers and divers. Water temperatures rarely rose above 70 degrees Fahrenheit and often were below 50 degrees on the surface. In the winter, temperatures reached the low '40s. Bill and Bob tried surfing with their old Army sweaters, wringing them out and putting them back on after almost every ride. That didn't work.

Wetsuits of the time, generally made for the military from thick rubber, were heavy, bulky, and uncomfortable, especially for the free-flowing movements of surfing. Bill and Bob tried electrically heated pilots' suits from military surplus, but their electrical wiring and battery power were major dangers for those wearing the suits in the ocean.

They realized that the world of diving was about to change, and they wanted in.

An opportunity presented itself when they teamed up with two local surfers who would later become world famous. Hap Jacobs, who pioneered the modern surfboard, and Bev Morgan, a renowned surfer and diver, had opened up a small surfing and diving shop in Redondo Beach called Dive N' Surf. Bev began making wetsuits for divers in the early 1950s. At the same time, Bill was talking with Dale Velzy, another local surfer, about going into the surfing business in Malibu. Bill talked Jacobs into going into the surfboard shaping business with Velzy and, with Velzy gone, the Meistrell brothers had a chance to buy into Dive N' Surf. When surfboard shaping moved out of the shop, much-needed space was freed up for the manufacturing of wetsuits.

Bev offered Bill a chance to buy in, and he said that he would only do it if his brother Bob could join them, and Bev agreed. With $1,800, largely borrowed from their mother, Bill and Bob became two-thirds owners of their first dive and surf business in 1953. Bev continued to make wetsuits, with Bill learning from him and beginning to conceive new designs and methods to improve the manufacturing process. Bob, always the more talkative of the two, worked sales in the shop.

(Left to right) Dale Velzy, Hap Jacobs, Bill and Bev (Bob took the picture)
in front of the original Dive N' Surf location.
Photo credit: Meistrell Archive

Because the business was so new, and struggling in the slowly developing surfing and diving industries, both Bill and Bob maintained their $75-a-month lifeguard jobs five days a week and worked at the shop the other two days. On their first day of business, Bob sold a Skin Diver magazine for 15 cents. Later that night, their mother asked them if they thought this was a good start. They thought it was, but added that sales would get better. They set a goal of $100 a day, while they kept their full-time lifeguard jobs. Gradually, they reached that goal, and achieved higher results each month by expanding their product lines and doing whatever they could to ramp up sales.

In 1958 they bought out Bev Morgan when he declared he wanted to go off on a surfing trip around the world. He had prepared a complete inventory sheet and presented it to Bill and Bob, seeking payment for a third of the total value he had determined. They told Bev they didn't have that kind of money, but Bev was adamant. He told them to write a check for the amount and give it to him, which they did. He signed the back of it and handed it back, saying all he wanted them to do was pay his monthly alimony while he was gone. That's how Bill and Bob learned Bev was getting divorced before he set out on his trip.

Bill (left) and Bob always gave good customer service.
Photo credit: Meistrell Archive

Bill, Bev and Bob in front of Dive N' Surf in an early ad in Skin Diver *magazine.*
Photo credit: Meistrell Archive

When Bob talked about this photo he said it was of him.
Bill said it was of him. Either way, one of them had a unique
experience swimming with a basking shark.
Photo credit: Meistrell Archive

Bill was usually in the back making wetsuits
while Bob was in the front selling them.
Photo credit: Meistrell Archive

Bill and Bob wasted no time moving Dive N' Surf forward. They realized that wetsuits were bought mostly by divers but, as surfers, they thought that surfers would buy their wetsuits if the suits were more flexible and comfortable. So they set out to make several design innovations. Plus, they planned to broaden their product base by adding bigger-ticket items.

At that time, most surf shops in the South Bay just sold surfboards. No one sold what Bill and Bob sold, which included spear guns, Boston Whaler skiffs, Johnson outboard motors, and a host of other items. They transformed the industry by adding a variety of products to make surfing and diving more enjoyable and safe.

Bob Evans, who started sweeping the floor and filling air tanks for Bill and Bob at the age of sixteen, said, "I should have had a camera when I worked there. It was like a reality show. You never knew what was going to happen."

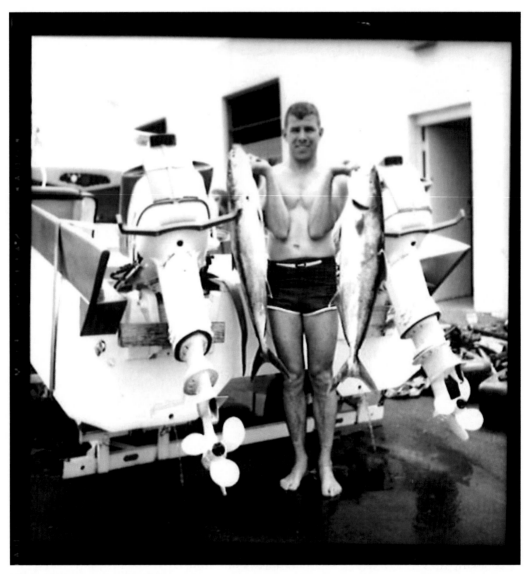

The brothers stayed true to their passion.
Bob after spearfishing off the coast.
Photo credit: Meistrell Archive

(Left to right) Bev, Bob Kulek, Bob, and Bill with their catch of the day.
Photo credit: Meistrell Archive

Evans said it was Bob Meistrell who got him started in his own business. "I always was making things, and Bob told me to make something beneficial. He said, 'Go make a better swim fin.' I did, and that was beginning of Force Fins."

Even though they tried to stay out of trouble, sometimes they got into a little mischief. Even the police were curious about what Bill and Bob were up to.
Photo credit: Meistrell Archive

Greg Noll: "Bobby and Billy created a successful business, but it came from their passion for surfing and diving, not their love of money. In the early days, they were so far into diving it was part of their life. They really became the two experts. They became the most knowledgeable divers in the whole area—kind of like the 'mini-Cousteaus' of the South Bay."

THE FIRST COMMERCIALLY VIABLE WETSUIT

6

After Bill and Bob joined Bev at Dive N' Surf, Bill knew they needed to find a better way to make more flexible wetsuits, and his goal was to find the right material. Bill heard of a company in Gardena, California, that had a rubber product he thought would be a better material for their wetsuits. He learned it was actually a synthetic rubber called neoprene, made by Rubatex, Inc., in Bedford, Virginia, and it wasn't long before Bill embarked on a forty-nine-hour car ride on a hunt to find the best material possible for wetsuits.

> The principle behind a wetsuit is fairly simple. Neoprene is a closed-cell foam. Within a thin sheet of neoprene are thousands of tiny bubbles, which form a barrier to keep body heat in and cold water out. When the suit gets wet, a thin layer of water seeps in and remains trapped inside, where it warms to the temperature of the body and creates an insulating layer between body and suit.

As he toured the Rubatex plant, Bill felt all of the rubber samples, and when he came to one smooth product he asked, "What's this?"

"That's what we call G-231," the company rep answered. "We sell it to Pontiac and all the car companies to make gaskets for the taillights on cars."

Recognizing that it would be just right for their wetsuits, Bill brought a few sheets of the G-231 rubber material back to Redondo Beach, where he and Bev started using it in their wetsuits. This closed-cell nitrogen-blown rubber material had better insulating quality and greater flexibility, making it the perfect material from which to make wetsuits for divers. Plus, thought Bill and Bob, if divers could benefit from this design, so could surfers.

Some of the ingredients to make the perfect wetsuit.
Photo credit: Body Glove International

A customer proudly wearing his Dive N' Surf wetsuit.
Photo credit: Body Glove International

Diane Kulek hard at work gluing wetsuits together.
Photo credit: Body Glove International

Shortly afterward, and to Bill's amazement, an order for one hundred wetsuits arrived from the US Navy's Underwater Demolition Team, which had heard about their new wetsuit material. Bill and Bob went down to San Diego and measured all of the personnel for their suits. When they returned they got busy making the suits, right after they took the $11,000 check to the bank. As Bill remembered later, "That was like big time, man."

Over the ensuing years, Dive N' Surf would become a major player in surfing and diving, with Bill and Bob at the center of the activity. They began in earnest manufacturing their neoprene wetsuits under the brand name Dive N' Surf "Thermocline." While surfers did not use wetsuits at that time, avid surfers Bill and Bob recognized the potential for wetsuits in surfing and set out to design and manufacture suits that would be attractive to surfers as well as divers.

As business took off, a full inventory of wetsuits was needed.

Greg Noll said, "I was kind of a hold out. I didn't like a lot of stuff around me, but eventually I caved in.

There were a lot of guys that were so used to not having wetsuits that when they came out, it was difficult to deal with the restriction and the rubber. But at that time wetsuits were a big deal. Wetsuits made a big difference!"

Greater sales demanded larger inventory.
Photo credit: Body Glove International

Dive N' Surf took the basic rubber wetsuit and made important and innovative design changes that made them more comfortable and warm. It became the first company to

- make a three-piece hood so it fit better.

- put a separate collar on the wetsuit. It wasn't just a seam, like other companies' wetsuits; it was a band all the way around the neck.

- use a V-design under the arms, which caused much less arm-pit rash by reducing the amount of rubbing against the skin.

- have a diamond shape in the crotch, which decreased the wear and tear. Prior models had four seams meeting in the crotch, but with the diamond design, wetsuits lasted longer.

- roll the neoprene at the cuffs on the legs and arms for a tighter seal at the feet and hands.

- glue the seams for longer wear.

- put plastic material on zippers so they could be sewn into place more easily.

- make hard-soled booties so surfers and divers could walk on the rocks. At that time the soft-sole bootie would not last at all on rocky ground.

- While Bill and Bob were making a normal size run of XS–XXL, they also invented a personal measurement chart with twenty-eight separate measurements so each wetsuit could be made to order with custom fitting.

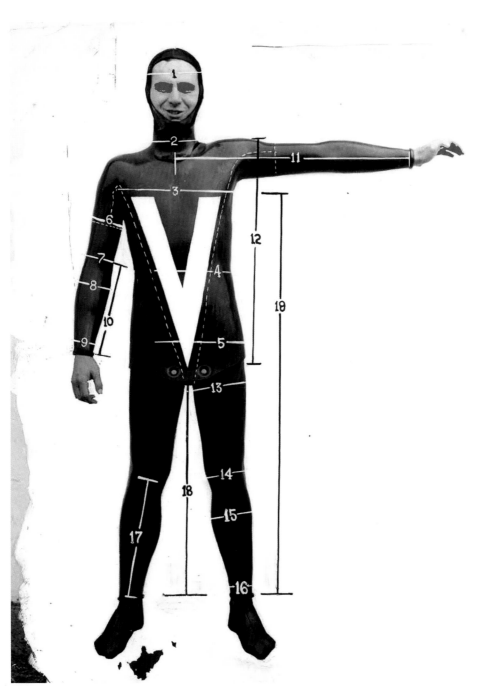

The first image the twins used to measure custom wetsuits.
Photo credit: Body Glove International

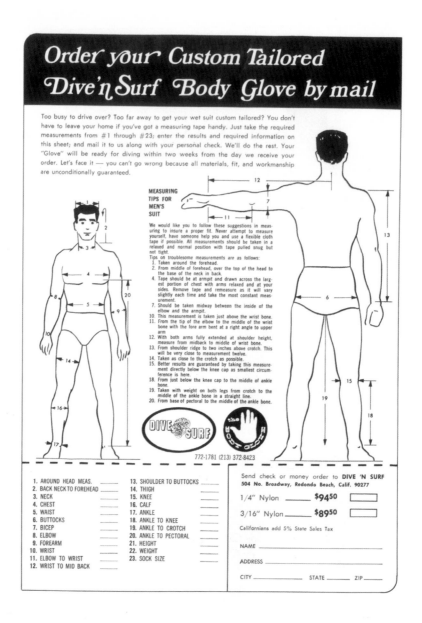

The original form that was used by customers to order a custom wetsuit.
Photo credit: Body Glove International

"In fact," recalled Hap Jacobs, "when I hadn't been surfing in a long time, I went back to get a wetsuit from Billy and he said, 'Well, just go in the restroom there and put one on and we'll see how it fits.' Okay. So I'm in there a long time and he says, 'What are you doing?' I said, 'I'm putting on a wetsuit.' He says, 'Where do you have the zipper?' When I said 'In front,' he started laughing and said, 'They're not in the front anymore. They're in the back.' And I went, 'Oh, geez, I've got to start all over!'"

Bill and Bob soon hired a local advertising representative, Duke Boyd, who was helping local surf shops build their brands. One of the first things Duke said was that the wetsuit brand name Dive N' Surf "Thermocline" was a terrible name, from a marketing and sales perspective. It was difficult to explain to potential customers what "Thermocline" meant (a layer of water separating warmer and cooler layers of water), and that didn't help sales.

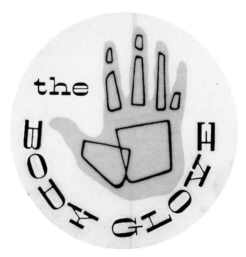

The original Body Glove logo.
Photo credit: Body Glove International

Boyd, who later gained fame as the creator of the Hang Ten and Lightning Bolt brands, asked Bill to describe the characteristics of the "Thermocline" suits. Bill's immediate reply that "They fit like a glove" was all Boyd had to hear. He told the start-up businessmen that their new brand should be Body Glove. In three days Duke returned with the new design of the now famous hand logo in black and gold, and an invoice. With $200 to Duke for the name and $35 to a logo designer, they were now in business as Body Glove, a name and a brand that would become world famous. It was 1965, and things were going to get a lot more exciting for Bill and Bob, Dive N' Surf, and the Body Glove brand.

7

DIVE INSTRUCTORS:
BUILT FOR LIFE

In the mid-1950s, Bill, Bob, and partner Bev Morgan were breaking new ground by creating an organized approach to scuba (self-contained underwater breathing apparatus) diving. They were seriously concerned for the safety of those who wanted to explore the world below the ocean's surface. The invention of the Aqua-Lung in 1943 by Frenchmen Jacques-Yves Cousteau and Emile Gagnan, which included the demand regulator invented by Gagnan, led to an increased interest in underwater diving. People were drawn to the oceans by the scuba gear and newly designed, more effective wetsuits. Bill, Bob, and Bev, as lifeguards and active divers, realized the

Bill and Bob's first monthly newsletter.
Photo code: Meistrell Archive

absolute necessity for quality training, and they set out to make it happen.

When Bill and Bob started diving, first as kids in Missouri and then more seriously as adults in California, they knew next to nothing about the biological and physical aspects of diving. The words decompression, air embolism, and equalization had not entered their vocabulary. Basically, what they knew about diving came through trial and error, with the emphasis on the errors. Bill and Bob often joked that it was a mystery to them how they hadn't died as a result of their underwater forays. Through the connection with Bev Morgan, though, they soon moved to change all that.

As Los Angeles County lifeguards, Bill, Bob, and Bev had seen their share of deaths caused by inexperienced and untrained divers not knowing how to handle emergencies underwater. They all agreed that a diving certification course was needed, and Bev convinced Los Angeles County that it also needed a diver training manual, which he was hired to write. Bob enrolled and was a member of the first instructor course known as UICC #1. Over the years he

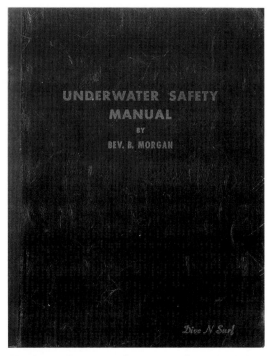

The first underwater safety manual for scuba divers. Photo credit: Bev Morgan

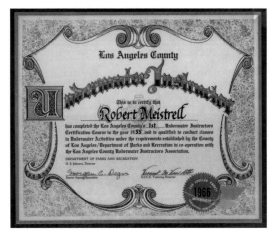

Bob's Underwater Instructor certificate in 1955. Photo credit: Meistrell Archive

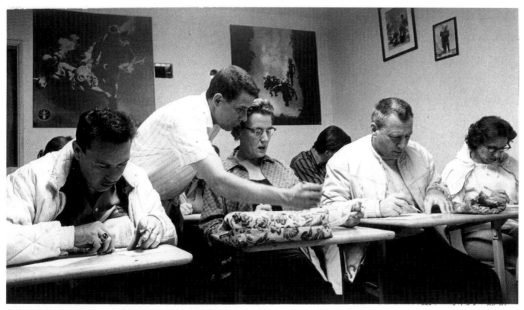

Bob teaching in the classroom in the 1960s.
Photo credit: Meistrell Archive

Bob in the classroom in the 1970s.
Photo credit: Meistrell Archive

would come to believe that the course and manual they created saved hundreds of lives by teaching essential dive procedures to new divers. As a new instructor, Bob taught classes at the Hermosa Plunge, the Biltmore Hotel, and at his friends Carl and Judy Grimes' house.

In 1958 an additional Dive N' Surf shop was built at 504 North Broadway in Redondo Beach with an indoor, heated pool for scuba classes. No other dive shop had an indoor pool for instruction at that time. In what was another first for the growing diving industry, customers were required to take the diving certification course Bill and Bob had created before they were allowed to leave the store with newly purchased equipment. For more than two years Dive N' Surf was the only dive shop with this requirement, but it was part of Bill and Bob's concern for the safety of new divers.

Over the ensuing years, Bob trained hundreds of divers. Bob certified more divers than Bill because he was more active in sales at the shop while Bill attended to the technical side of the business. Bob was very demanding as an instructor and required his students to accomplish a number of actions that no other dive instructors did.

Bob taught as if his students' lives depended on what he taught—and they did. He didn't want to teach people only how to pass a certification test—which he believed anyone could teach—but how to survive underwater, where anything could, and often did, go wrong.

Because he knew that divers would need to clear their masks, he taught students how to remove their masks underwater five times with one hand.

Dive N' Surf shop where the indoor pool was located.
Photo credit: Meistrell Archive

Dive N' Surf original ad in Skin Diver *magazine.*
Photo credit: Meistrell Archive

JOHNSON MOTORS
BOSTON WHALERS
MARINE HARDWARE
SCUBA INSTRUCTIONS
SKIN DIVING EQUIPMENT

DIVE N' SURF
INC

BOB MEISTRELL

p.o. box 511
504 n. broadway   •   redondo beach, ca. 90277
213 - 372-8423   •   213 - 772-1781

Original Dive N' Surf business card.
Photo credit: Meistrell Archive

Bob enjoying one of his favorite past times: teaching.
Photo credit: Meistrell Archive

He had students take off their fins and hang upside down on the pool coping while they cleared their mask and mouthpiece. He showed them that the mouthpiece would still work if they turned it 180 degrees while they were suspended upside down.

Bob always taught students that the best thing they could do for themselves when confronted by an emergency under water was to take a moment to figure out a solution rather than rushing to the surface in a panic.

He taught them how to stay calm and confident in situations where most people would lose their cool.

Part of what made Bob a great instructor was his attention to detail.
Photo credit: Meistrell Archive

Bob had his students exhale completely to feel what it was like under water. He told them that one of the safest
descents is to go down feet first along
an anchor chain. And, in case they lost
a fin while diving, he had them remove
a fin to feel how hard it was to swim
with all of their gear.

He had students tread water for a
long time with their gear on and then

Bob in the 1960s teaching student how to use a
regulator.
Photo credit: Meistrell Archive

Bob (far right) teaching students before they take their first breath underwater.
Photo credit: Meistrell Archive

swim around the Dive N' Surf pool walls. He would also have them swim two laps underwater without wearing a mask. He taught them pressure equalization techniques. To be certified by Bob, one had to attend five or six classroom and pool sessions.

Bob was the first to provide both beach and boat dives before certification. Others solely required a beach dive, which usually meant shallow water only. When he finally handed his students their certification card after their last dive, he was comfortable knowing that they had become capable scuba divers.

Bill and Bob next to Dive N' Surf Demonstrator that was used to take customers out.
Photo credit: Meistrell Archive

Dive N' Surf also was the first company to have its own air compressor, an impressively large machine that took up its own room at the Broadway Street location. Bought in 1958, it was a military surplus compressor from the 1940s that was so well built that it was still operational when the Dive N' Surf building was renovated recently. While there were repairs to the compressor over the past fifty-five years, the machine was never rebuilt. It was replaced in 2013 and is now is on display as part of Dive N' Surf/Body Glove history in a building across Broadway.

The new compressor is actually three compressors in one large unit: two high-pressure breathing air compressors and one Nitrox compressor system. The two high-pressure compressors are identical Bauer models that have computer controllers with a touch screen control menu display. Pressure transducers are used to monitor and

Original Dive N' Surf tank filling stations. The one on right served until 2013 Dive N' Surf remodeling.
Photo credit: Meistrell Archive

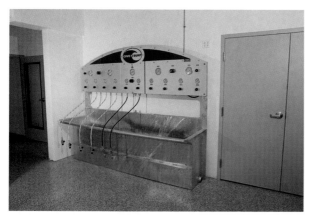

The new filling station at Dive N' Surf.
Photo credit: Body Glove International

control the compressors' start and stop function. This system includes the most current compressor technology in the world today. The total capacity with both compressors operating is 84 CFM (cubic feet per minute), which will fill a dive tank in sixty seconds or sixty tanks per hour. This impressively short time to fill a tank means that customers will never have to wait more than a minute or two for their tanks to be filled.

The Nitrox compressor is from Brownie's Marine Group in Florida. Nitrox, also known as enriched air nitrox, has an oxygen content above the normal 21 percent contained in air and is mainly used in scuba diving to extend bottom time and reduce the risk of decompression sickness.

Just as, in the 1960s, Dive N' Surf's dive-training programs, indoor pool, and state-of-the-art compressor attracted would-be divers, who signed up for training and certification, so today the new compressor is attracting divers from throughout California and across the country.

8

LIFESTYLE BECOMES INCOME

Dive N' Surf was still not making a profit after Bill and Bob bought in, so Bev and the twins continued to work as lifeguards. Bob remembers they agreed that if they could just get the sales up to $100 a day they'd have a nice little business. They weren't taking anything out of the company, choosing instead to pour everything back into it to make it stronger. Over time, the sales increased from $100 to well into the thousands in the late 1960s.

During this time, Bob, with a wife and son to care for, worked numerous side jobs to bring money home. He cleaned various businesses at night in Manhattan Beach, including Bentley's, Lee's Fashions, and Joe's Candy Cottage. Then he got up early in the morning, sometimes at three-thirty,

Bob tending to his shop.
Photo credit: Meistrell Archive

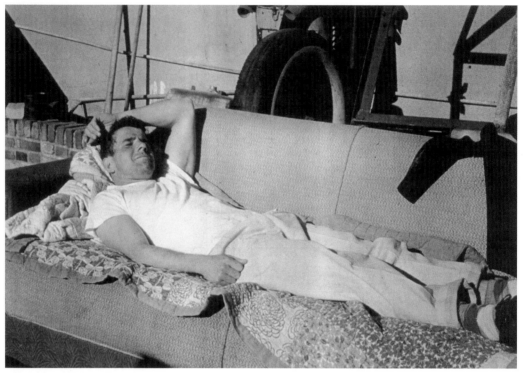

Bill taking a nap during one of his 15-hour workdays.
Photo credit: Meistrell Archive

and went to Pancho's, where he helped clean the restaurant. After coffee and breakfast, he'd surf for a while and then report to El Porto lifeguard station for a nine-to-five shift, followed by time at home with his family before starting all over again.

Bill worked at outside jobs, too, including at a bicycle shop, and contin-

Bill (left) and Bob getting ready to dive with saturated gas, something they were testing.
Photo credit: Don Siverts

Diving experiment with saturated gas

Bill wearing high-tech diving equipment for the era.
Photo credit: Don Siverts

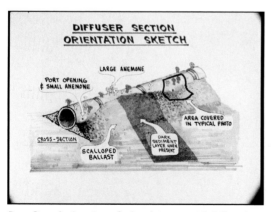

DIFFUSER SECTION ORIENTATION SKETCH

LARGE ANEMONE

PORT OPENING & SMALL ANEMONE

CROSS-SECTION

SCALLOPED BALLAST

DARK SEDIMENT LAYER WHEN PRESENT

AREA COVERED IN TYPICAL PHOTO

Don Sivert's drawing of what he saw with Bill and Bob while diving along the pipe.
Photo credit: Don Siverts

ued his lifeguard service to help make ends meet while building the dive and surf business.

Bill and Bob wanted to make more money, so when Bill Parson from the Los Angeles County Sanitation Department called to ask them to do some diving for the department, they eagerly said yes. Parson wanted them to dive and inspect several underwater pipes that were 75 and 90 inches wide. He told them the pipes were as deep as 225 feet down in the ocean.

They didn't know much about deep diving, but they started doing the work for the Sanitation Department. Bill and Bob went to the shop at five in the morning and waited for a phone call from Parsons. They did several 225-foot dives without lead weight belts or buoyancy compensators. They wore two air tanks and just battled their way down along the pipe. At about 100 feet their wetsuits would compress and their tanks, filled with air, weighed 6 pounds, so they would simply free fall to the end of the pipe.

Some days the water was so clear they could see 200 feet horizontally. But, even though the surface water

Bill and Bob, deep dive 225 feet
to check sanitation pipes

Photos of Bill and Bob prepping for the dive, the sanitation pipe,
and diving along the pipe.
Photo credit: Don Siverts

temperature was 69 degrees, the water at the bottom was 42 degrees. They knew they had to figure a way to stay warm if they were going to be able to do the work.

Their plan was ingenious. They captured hot water from their boat's exhaust system and put it into black bags, which they stuffed into their wetsuit, thereby making personal water bottles. This allowed them to do the inspections in relative comfort. From the money earned for these dives, they were able to buy new equipment, including a newly designed regulator with a stainless steel diaphragm.

Bob remembered one dive with Don Siverts when they were taking pictures of a pipe at a depth of 175 feet when Bob's air supply cut off completely. As he described it, "No reserve, no nothing!" Bob hit the regulator with his dive knife, but nothing happened. He signaled Don that he was in trouble.

While they had another air tank and regulator on the bottom, it was too far in what Bob called the wrong direction. He wanted to go to the surface, not the bottom. So they ascended, with Bob and Don "buddy breathing" with Don's mouthpiece. At 40 feet they released their emergency buoy, but their safety diver in the boat was not paying attention and didn't see the buoy.

After staying at 40 feet a while longer, they made their way to the surface and, after a few words with their safety diver, he brought extra tanks to them at the 40-foot depth. They did extra decompression and arrived back at their boat in good condition.

Bob took the regulator back to the manufacturer and showed them that the so-called stainless steel diaphragm was actually tin, and it had simply folded under and stopped the breathing of the regulator. These were the trial and error moments that were pivotal at the beginning of the dive industry. This problem could have meant certain death for Bob, but knowing how to buddy breathe with his dive buddy Don saved his life.

A while later, Bill and Bob were asked by a representative of the Southern California Edison Electric Company if they did commercial diving. Bob said they did inspections, but not construction-related diving. The company rep said he had half-mile-long underwater intake and outflow tunnels along the coast, 17 feet in diameter, that he wanted Bill and Bob to swim through.

Bob asked, "What's the purpose for going through the tunnels?"

And the man said, "To see if you can do it."

Bob said, "I don't think that is very damn funny," but they went down to look at where they would go in and come out.

Having determined that the greatest depth of the tunnels was about 40 feet, they measured off a half mile on the ocean and swam it a number of times to determine how long it took to go that distance at that depth. They estimated that, even doing the inspection, it should take about forty-eight minutes to swim through a tunnel and back.

As a safety precaution, and no doubt remembering Bob's close call with the faulty regulator, they bolted together a double tank and a single tank to create a three-tank configuration, each tank holding 72 cubic feet of air. A breathing hose ran from the double tanks to their mouthpiece, and a single hose ran from the single tank. That way, if they ran into trouble with the double tanks or regulator, they could easily remove the double tank hose and insert the hose from the single tank. No one had done this before. Once more, Bill and

Bob (left) and Bill with the gear they used on their deep dives.
Photo credit: Meistrell Archive

The three-tank combination Bill and Bob used on their deep dives.
Photo credit: Body Glove International

Bill and Bob before their dived through the tunnel.
Photo Credit: Don Siverts

Bob were exploring new territory as they gained diving experience in a variety of environments and unique conditions that demanded ingenuity from them.

The night before the inspection of the first tunnel, they thought about all the things that could go wrong, including the power company reversing the flow of the water through the tunnels, thereby trapping them inside. Despite the risks, they decided they could do the inspections safely, and maybe even make a bunch of money.

On their first dive into the tunnels, they jumped from the Redondo Beach breakwater and swam down to the tunnel entrance. This first time wasn't productive because there was current inside the tunnel, which caused them to tumble and restricted their ability to see anything. They didn't even charge the power company for the dive.

After having the electric company stop the current, which was created by large impellers that either drew salt water in to cool the electric generators or pulled the heated water back out, they dove again and immediately realized that if they got turned around inside the tunnels it would be impossible to tell which way to swim because compasses didn't work inside the metal tunnels. They decided to wear enough weights to be able to plant their feet on the bottom and make impressions of their fins in the direction they were supposed to swim. This became standard procedure for all divers afterwards.

Bob often told a funny story about the intake and outflow impellers. He asked a power company employee how they started the huge impellers that move the water in the tunnels. When the man pointed to two keys on a control board and said that both keys had to be turned simultaneously, Bob took one of the keys and kept it with him when he dove.

Because Southern California Edison decided to put the diving operation out to bid, some other divers won the next contract on a low bid. Bill and Bob told them to wear enough weights to make impressions in the bottom of the pipes, but they refused to heed that advice. Wearing regular weight belts, they soon realized the error of their ways when they became disoriented and wasted most of their air trying to figure out how to get out of the tunnel alive. Bill and Bob never had to bid again.

Once Bill and Bob had inspected the tunnels and submitted pictures and reports to Southern California Edison, the company stopped dive inspections because it couldn't get insurance for such dangerous operations. But, once again, Bill and Bob had taken on a new adventure, figured out how to do it safely, and accomplished the task. With the dives earning them about $1,000 per day, they also made much-needed money to support their business and families.

Life and business were looking up for the Meistrell twins. They expanded their product lines by becoming a dealer for both Boston Whaler boats and Johnson outboard motors. These were major investments in their future that would, in time, prove to be extremely beneficial. In their inimitable style, Bill and Bob realized that these two manufacturers could add significant income streams to their business, but it would require additional work and education for both men. As an example of their commitment to this expanded direction, Bill arranged to attend the Johnson Motor Company's mechanic school in Waukegan, Illinois. In March 1958, he and Jackie drove across the country for the week-long school. Bill started classes immediately, and Jackie stayed in the car with the heater on until they found a motel that evening for the rest of their stay. Married to Bill for a couple of years at the time, Jackie well understood Bill's strong desire to learn as much as he could about how things worked, in this case Johnson outboard motors, so he could offer high quality customer service.

Coupled with their commitment to Johnson Motors, Bill and Bob's decision to become a Boston Whaler dealer made great financial sense. In a very short time, they became the largest Whaler dealer west of the Mississippi. Dive N' Surf was making big waves in the diving and surfing world, and California was beginning to take notice.

Bill (fourth from left) with his classmates at the Johnson Motor School.
Photo credit: Meistrell Archive

9

THE REAL "SURF CITY"

What became known as the surfing culture in the 1970s and '80s was just getting started in California in the early 1950s. There weren't yet movies, like Gidget, with surfing themes or backgrounds. But there was a lot of surfing activity all along the California coast, especially in the South Bay area below Los Angeles. Manhattan Beach, Hermosa Beach, and Redondo Beach were becoming hot spots for surfing, and an entire culture was beginning.

Bill in mid-winter before the wetsuit.
Photo credit: Meistrell Archive

Hawaiian surfer George Freeth introduced surfing to California in 1907. Over the ensuing years a few local surfers discovered a number of surfing locales that became popular as the sport caught on. While surfing didn't expand much in the '30s and '40s, the period after the Korean War was an entirely different story. Young Californian men who had been in the military during

Korea returned home to their favorite beaches and boards. It was as if their absence had created an even greater interest in surfing.

The late 1940s and the 1950s were a pivotal time in the South Bay for the advancement of the surf culture. South Bay surfers gained reputations for their inventive moves and aggressive rides. Surfboards began to shrink in size as the Californians put aside their traditional Hawaiian long boards to experiment with various materials and designs, all in the search for the best board to catch the best wave. A few of the surfers became recognized for their individual surfing styles.

The first surfboards were between 9 and 11 feet long and made of balsa and redwood. With the advent of fiberglass technology during World War II, however, fiberglass came into favor with a few board makers in the South Bay area, notably Preston "Pete" Peterson. He is credited with making the first fiberglass surfboard in 1946.

In 1949 Bob Simmons created the "sandwich" surfboard, which had a foam core encased in plywood, along with balsa wood outer rails and a coating of fiberglass for waterproofing.

Bronze bust of George Freeth on the Redondo Beach Pier.
Photo credit: Body Glove International

Torrance Beach on a sunny summer day in the 1950s.
Photo credit: Meistrell Archive

A typical day at the beach between surfs.
Photo credit: Meistrell Archive

Patty Meistrell holding her personalized surfboard in front of the Hermosa Beach Biltmore Hotel.
Photo credit: Meistrell Archive

Surfboards were evolving rapidly as the 1950s opened.

Hap Jacobs recalled when his family moved to the beach in the early '40s and he was introduced to surfing by local kids. In high school he got a job sweeping and cleaning surf mats at a local attraction, where he also got to ride the mats before and after regular hours. That's where he met Bill and Bob, as well as Dale Velzy and others who later became well known in the surfing community.

Hap went to Hawaii to surf, returning to South Bay two years later with a wife. "There came a time when I actually had to figure out how I was going to make some money," he said. In 1952, he and Bev Morgan were surfing a lot together and Bev was experimenting with wetsuit manufacturing, during what Hap called the "Neanderthal stage" of wetsuits because they were so basic.

Hap and Bev decided to work together to make wetsuits and surfboards, so in 1953 they established a small business they called, aptly enough, "Dive N' Surf." Situated in a small shop at 223 Hermosa Avenue in Redondo Beach, right at the beach, they were so close to the ocean that waves sometimes splashed onto the back of the building.

But Bev and Hap soon realized that making wetsuits out of rubber and making surfboards out of wood were incompatible activities. Wetsuits required glue, and surfboards required the balsa and redwood to be sanded during shaping. Doing both in the same shop, they were ending up with a smelly, sticky mess.

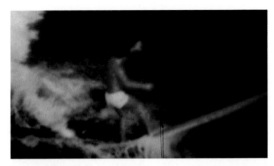

Bob surfing one of his favorite spots, Manhattan Beach Pier.
Photo credit: Meistrell Archive

Bill and Bob visited Dive N' Surf and showed an interest in making wetsuits. Bill talked with Dale Velzy, who was making surfboards, and suggested that Velzy talk with Hap Jacobs about joining him in surfboard manufacturing. Hap had orders for six boards, and Bev told him that Velzy did also, figuring Hap would see the wisdom of joining up with Velzy. Soon, Hap left Dive N' Surf to team up with Velzy in what became "Surfboards by Velzy and Jacobs." The path into Dive N' Surf was now open for Bill and Bob.

> *Hap said he and Velzy figured one guy would work the shop while the other surfed, but that didn't work out because they locked the door and they both went surfing!*

Beside Hap Jacobs and Dale Velzy, several other South Bay surfers emerged as the big names of the time. Bing Copeland, Dewey Weber, Rick Stoner, and Greg Noll became well known in California and soon opened surf shops in the South Bay. Copeland opened Bing's Surfboards, Dewey Weber created Dewy Weber Surfboards, and Greg Noll established Greg Noll Surfboards. While these talented surfers ventured fully into business, they always found time for their passion.

After Bill and Bob bought into Dive N' Surf, they began to sell their newly designed wetsuits to the surf shops operated by surfing's cream of the crop, even private-labeling wetsuits for other surf shops, too. Soon Greg Noll, Mickey Munoz, Jeff Hakman, David Nuuhiwa, Hobart "Hobie" Alter, Gerry Lopez, Mike Purpus, Robert August, and Larry Bertlemann had Dive N' Surf "Thermocline" wetsuits.

Hobie Alter and Mickey Munoz featured in Dive N' Surf ad in Surfer *magazine.*
Photo credit: Body Glove International

Several other surfers from this period became famous, including Bob Simmons, Joe Quigg, Sonny Vardeman, Terry Tracy, Mike Doyle, Mickey Dora, and a host of others. The Southern California surfing culture was underway. Bill and Bob were a significant part of its creation and they would play an even bigger role in its transition into a national and international phenomenon.

Despite claims to the contrary from both Huntington Beach and Santa Cruz, California, the South Bay area of Los Angeles County is the original locale of the true "Surf City." Even though Huntington Beach and Santa Cruz actually went into court to battle out which would use the official title "Surf City USA," with Huntington Beach winning, there is no question in the minds of early California surfers where the California surf culture really began.

When George Freeth left Hawaii for Redondo Beach, where he became a lifeguard in the South Bay, he was hired by developer Henry Huntington to put on a surfing demonstration at the end of the railroad line in Redondo Beach to market the beach community and

Surfing at its peak in Hermosa Beach.
Photo credit: Meistrell Archive

Jackie Meistrell on the Redondo Beach Boardwalk.
Photo credit: Meistrell Archive

get people to ride his railroad down to the beach. For the most part it worked, until the rail lines were washed away by the local surf in the always-changing beach area of Manhattan, Hermosa, and Redondo Beaches.

> Hap Jacobs: "I'd known Bill and Bob for years, just from being at the beach and then they were lifeguards at Hermosa pier. They were always surfing by the pier."

When one talks with South Bay surfers of the '40s and '50s, they vividly remember surfing in their own "backyard." The surf lifestyle and culture sprang from South Bay and then spread to Huntington Beach in the south and Santa Cruz to the north.

Patty Meistrell in a "Queen of the Beach" contest in Hermosa Beach.
Photo credit: Meistrell Archive

All of the Southern California surfers from the early days repeat the same sentiment: South Bay was where it all started. Mike Purpus said it best: "Hermosa Beach and the whole South Bay was the original 'Surf City.'"

In the South Bay, this was never an issue because surfers were just trying to figure out how to get a board, and eventually a wetsuit, so they could enjoy life in the new surfing culture. The beach lifestyle attracted young people from communities all along the coast. Hap Jacobs remembers that there were lots of groups of young surfers at various places, such as Twenty-Second, Twen-

Bill and Bob with friends about to paddle out.
Photo credit: Meistrell Archive

ty-Fourth, and Twenty-Sixth Streets, and at both Manhattan and Hermosa Piers, where the waves were great.

New words joined the surfers' language: the "groms" or "grommets" were kids, older surfers were "locals," and the best surfer was the "kahuna" or "boss." Mickey Dora was even called the "King"!

Bob with his Simmons slot bottom surfboard in the early 1950s.
Photo credit: Meistrell Archive

A collection of surfboards from the 1950s.
Photo credit: Meistrell Archive

In Manhattan Beach, local lifeguards, including Bill and Bob, and local firemen donated money so the young surfers could build a clubhouse to sleep in, under the Manhattan Beach Pier. They bought wood and built what became the Manhattan Beach Surf Club. The local authorities must have thought it was better for the young surfers to have a fixed place under the pier than to sleep all over the beaches.

When Bev Morgan got involved in surfing in Manhattan Beach, he hung out with Greg Noll, Bing Copeland, and Bob Hogan. He had a license to drive at fourteen, so he surfed up and down the coast with Bing and Greg. Then Bob Simmons started shaping boards, and they all hung around him and Dale Velzy.

Bob Simmons was one of the original surfboard craftsmen who came from South Bay. He experimented with new and different materials, such as fiberglass, to make surfboards lighter and easier to turn. He produced the first twin fin surfboard to go on the market. The Simmons 1950 twin fin slot bottom that Bob bought in 1952 is still owned by the Meistrell family. Bob purchased it from Simmons for $75 and today it is worth tens of thousands of dollars. The board is an early design, but one that shows Simmons was far ahead of his time in crafting new ideas for surf equipment. Hap Jacobs recalls that Bev, Bill, and Bob were all riding Simmons boards at Hermosa Pier.

Many more surfboard shapers followed Simmons in the '60s. Notable among them were Dale Velzy, Hap Jacobs, Bing Copeland, Greg Noll, and Dewey Weber. Hap recalls that at the time he and Velzy joined up to make surfboards, others in the area were Dave Sweet, Greg Noll working out of a garage, and Hobie Alter down in Dana Point.

A fascinating part of the South Bay culture was the continuum of innovative new products to make their surf experience that much better. Mike Purpus recalls, "The first wetsuit made for surfing, and which was actually worn by surfers, was the one made by Bev Morgan and the Meistrells." The Meistrell twins, along with Bev Morgan, were heavily engaged in finding better materials to make wetsuits.

Hap Jacobs recalls one cold night he and Velzy went into the ocean at the Hermosa Pier after a rainstorm. "The wind was blowing hard, it was freezing, nobody was at the beach, but the waves were really good. A friend showed up who was a good surfer, but he wouldn't wear a wetsuit. Velzy and I had on ours as we paddled out. The friend turned purple before he finally returned to shore and went home. Later, we called his house and spoke with his mom, who said she was concerned about her son, who she'd been taking hot water to in the bathtub since he came home two hours before. Wetsuits were the thing!"

Not only were there great craftsmen who came from the South Bay area, but the original surfers were very talented surfers, as well. They pioneered a new generation of surf enthusiasts who traveled to Hawaii and found big waves beyond their wildest expectations. They met the great surfers of Hawaii, such as Duke Paoa Kahanamoku, Rabbit Kekai, and the Kealana and Aikau families. This sort of tribal reunion would take place year after year in the '60s.

None of them had money, but they loved surfing so much they figured out ways to make ends meet. When they were in Hawaii, they would free dive for fresh seafood.

When they were in the South Bay, they worked together to sell surfboards, wetsuits, T-shirts, and wax, all the while getting as much time surfing as they could. It was a great life for those who were part of the early days of surfing, with many of them moving into surfboard manufacturing.

10

DIVING AND SURFING MEET HOLLYWOOD

During sixty years with Body Glove, the Meistrells taught a large number of movie and television actors and actresses how to dive. Often, their families also were taught. Here are just some of the famous who came to Bill and Bob in the early days.

In 1956, Bob got an interesting phone call. The woman on the phone said, "We'd like to take a diving class." Bob asked, "Dive classes?" and she replied, "No, we just want to take one dive class. My husband and I don't have time to take a whole bunch of them."

Bob told the caller that he wouldn't teach just one class and that she would have to take several classes, including a beach dive and a boat dive. The lady said, "Well, we don't have time for that."

Bob told her that she really didn't have time to learn to dive if she didn't have the time to learn to do it properly. "I can teach you to dive in five minutes, but I can't teach you how to survive in five minutes, so you have to go through the whole series of classes."

She asked, "Do you know where we can take just one class?" and Bob said, "My competitor down the street teaches a one-class course in diving certification." The woman asked why Bob would recommend someone who taught a one-class course, and Bob said he wasn't recommending the guy, he was just answering her question.

The insistent woman told Bob they were going to buy a lot of diving equipment, to which Bob replied, "I'm not going to sell you any scuba equipment until I'm convinced you're going to be a good, safe, certified diver." Then, to Bob's surprise, she said, "I think we want to take classes with you. Would you come up to Los Angeles and teach us?" Bob answered that he didn't drive into Los Angeles because he had asthma and the smog made him miserable.

The woman said she and her husband actually lived in Bel Air, and Bob said he could go there because the air was cleaner, as befitting the city's name. She asked if he were married and then invited him to bring his wife, Patty, with him when he came to teach them to dive. Bob asked the lady's name and she said, "Rocky Cooper. Mrs. Gary Cooper."

When Bob and Patty drove up to the address Bob had been given, they were astonished to see Gary Cooper, the famous Hollywood actor, hand-washing his Bentley automobile. Cooper offered to help carry the tanks and other gear, but Bob said he'd handle it. All together, Bob held ten classes in the pool with the Coopers and their friends at their Bel Air home, and every night he'd be treated to a nice dinner. Bob remembers the Coopers as being "regular people" who, after they got to know you, were very warm and friendly. At first, Gary Cooper was shy and wouldn't say much, but after he got to know someone he opened up and even joked a lot.

Bob remembered a story Cooper told at dinner one night on his boat, the Portola, while anchored off Catalina Island.

An old sea captain was on this boat for years and years and years, and every morning he'd get up and come up to the pilot house. And he'd go over to the safe, and he'd dial the combination, and he'd pull out a little black box. He'd take a key from around his neck, and he'd open up the box, look into it, slam it down, and say, 'OK, I'm ready to go,' and he'd shut the safe.

So everybody wanted to know what he was looking at, but nobody would ask him. Then one day he died, and someone took the key from around his neck and he no sooner hit the water than they cut the safe open with a blowtorch and opened up the box with the key. On a piece of paper was written, 'Port is to the left; starboard is to the right.'

In 1958, movie producer Ivan Tors called Bill and asked him to bring Bob up to Hollywood to watch a television pilot Tors was making. After watching it, Bill and Bob predicted it would be the world's biggest show. As diving instructors, they told Tors there were tons of mistakes related to diving practices. Ivan Tors said, "Bob, it doesn't matter, only ten percent of the population knows how to dive." Bob wished that at least 1 percent actually knew how to dive. In the end, Ivan knew he should have listened to Bob as he had to go back and re-film a lot of scenes to make them correct.

Shortly thereafter, Walt Hoffman, who at that time was in charge of wardrobe for the television show Sea Hunt, called and said, "I'm going to bring Lloyd Bridges down and I want you to build him a rubber suit." Bill's instant reply was, "Well, come on down."

Hoffman and Bridges drove down to Redondo Beach and Bill measured Bridges for his wetsuit. A few days later, Bridges returned to try on the suit and, turning to Bill, said, "Billy, can you give me a little French cut here?" Bill had no idea what a French cut was, but he knew that anything having French cuts would make the suit look like a sissy suit, and that's what he told Lloyd Bridges.

Hoffman said to Bill, "Come here." He looked directly at Bill and said, "Billy, showbiz." Bill got it, and said, "Okay, showbiz." And he made Lloyd Bridges the suit he wanted, plus a couple more over the next few days. The suits were about $100 each, plus $100 to paint each suit, but that is a story yet to be told.

Bill and Bob later learned that Lloyd Bridges, despite his television character on Sea Hunt being a diver and all-around water personality, did not know how to dive. Bridges drove down to Redondo Beach to talk to Bob and figure out how he was going to learn how to dive.

"Listen, Bobby," he said, "I've got a real problem. I keep getting asked to go diving with dive clubs because they think I know how, but I don't." He was embarrassed to have to make up excuses for why he couldn't dive with them, and he had tired of the deception.

Bob agreed to teach Bridges how to dive, and also taught his sons Beau and Jeff.

The painted wetsuits arose from Sea Hunt's producers wanting Lloyd Bridges's wetsuits to be gray so they would be very different from standard black wetsuits. Bill and Bob used a gray glue so it would show up on television. They had to get really creative to give Lloyd Bridges his gray wetsuits, something that had never existed before.

Bill and Bob knew that when the neoprene sheets were made in a mold, a silicone powder residue remained on both sides of the material. When they had Johnny Hickham, a nephew who was the same size as Bridges, get into the wetsuit, they had to wipe the outside of the suit with toluene to remove the powder. Once it was clean, they painted it gray. Hickham then had to stand still for an hour with his arms straight out,

Bill with Lloyd Bridges.
Photo credit: Body Glove International

One of the gray wetsuits worn on the set of Sea Hunt.
Photo credit: Body Glove International

Robbie Meistrell helps Lloyd Bridges try on new gear.
Photo credit: Body Glove International

Bob assisting Gary Cooper into the water.
Photo credit: Body Glove International

holding on to two vertical poles, to allow the paint to dry. The last step was to coat the outside of the suit with talcum powder so the painted surfaces wouldn't stick together when Hickham lowered his arms and the material on the arms came into contact with the body of the suit.

Producer Ivan Tors asked how much Bill and Bob were charging for the suits. They said $100, and Tors said they'd do it themselves at the studio to save money. Well, the studio's wetsuit guy ended up with his arms and legs stuck together and they had to cut him out of the wetsuit because Bill and Bob "had forgotten" to tell Ivan Tors about the talcum powder covering they had found to be critical. They got the job back after that.

This may have been the first time Bill and Bob had painted a wetsuit, but it wasn't the last. It wouldn't be long before another studio wanted painted wetsuits, and soon production wetsuits would become available in various colors. But Bill and Bob were the first to do it.

Bob met Charlton Heston at the MGM Studios in Hollywood, where Heston was starring in the movie *The*

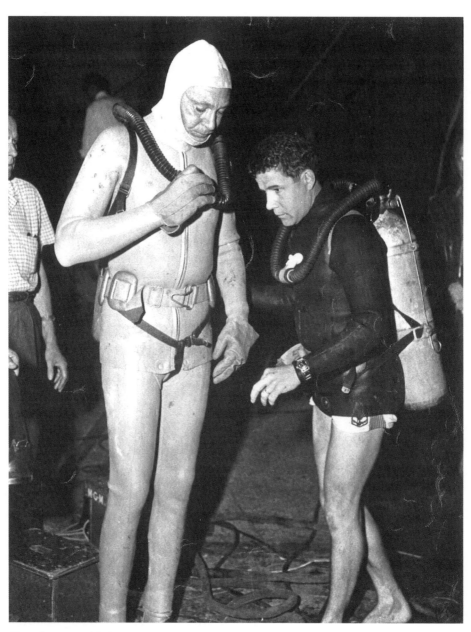

Gary Cooper and Bob on set.
Photo credit: Body Glove International

BOB MEISTRELL ASSISTS GARY COOPER
ON THE SET OF
THE WRECK OF THE MARY DEARE

Bob and Gary Cooper about to get into the water on the set of
The Wreck of the Mary Deare.
Photo credit: Body Glove International

Wreck of the Mary Deare at the time. Bob was the water safety consultant on the film for Gary Cooper. He remembered Heston as a really nice person who was easy to train in diving procedures. Gary and Rocky invited Heston, Bob, and tennis great Tony Trabert to travel with them to Catalina on their boat, the Portola.

One day in 1958, Bill was watching a football game on television when he got a telephone call. "Hey, this is Walt Hoffman and I want you to meet me at the corner of Lankershim and Rodeo Drive. We're going to Rudd Weatherwax's house to build a suit." Bill knew that Weatherwax was the animal trainer who had trained the original Lassie, canine hero of the Lassie movie. Bill said, "No, I won't build it. That dog won't wear a rubber suit!"

But they met and went to Weatherwax's home, where they found about eight "Lassies" all over the place. When Weatherwax introduced himself to Bill, Bill said, "We're going to measure your dog for a rubber suit," and Rudd said, "My dog doesn't wear a rubber suit." Bill looked at Hoffman, who said, "Well, then, we'll just have to get twelve suits—in large, medium, and small—but for people, so Lassie doesn't drown."

Hoffman was worried that Lassie might drown during a filming, but he settled on the crew standing off-camera wearing wetsuits in case they had to jump into cold water to save the dog. Bill, relieved he was going to make suits for people and not for dogs, recalled, "I made a good sale of suits that day. Kept us busy for a long time."

Bill and Bob made Raquel Welch a wetsuit for the movie Fantastic Voyage in 1966. In this movie, Stephen Boyd, Raquel Welch, and Donald Pleasence were to be miniaturized and, in a tiny submarine, injected into the vein of a person, with the purpose of fixing a blood clot before escaping from the body and returning to normal size.

Natalie Wood also was measured for a wetsuit, but Bill and Bob lost her measurements. She asked if they were doing it just to see her. Bill measured her and Bob wrote down the measurements, explaining that they needed more measurements to make the suit right, but in reality they simply had lost them. At least, that is the story they stuck with through all the years.

Bob helps Natalie Wood put on gear before a dive.
Photo credit: Body Glove International

This connection with the stars of Hollywood movies and television shows continued into the '80s and '90s, when *Baywatch* came calling in 1989. Producers needed wetsuits and related gear for the pilot of a proposed series about Los Angeles County lifeguards. They knew how much movie and television work Bill and Bob had done over the years, so they asked Body Glove for help. They saw Body Glove as the first and most prominent surfing and diving brand, so it was natural for them to call.

In an interesting twist, the person who called Body Glove was Michael Hoffman, son of Walt Hoffman, who knew exactly where to go. Michael's dad had worked with Bill and Bob on earlier productions, including Lassie, and the younger Hoffman soon worked closely with Bob's son, Randy, on *Baywatch*.

The company provided wetsuits, surfboards, bathing suits, and even T-shirts and volleyball shorts, all with the Body Glove logo prominently displayed. After the huge success of the pilot, the show began what would become a twelve-year run as the most watched television program in history. *Baywatch's* immense success in the United States was eclipsed by the size of its international audiences, and this achievement contributed greatly to the expansion of the Body Glove brand into foreign markets.

Each week millions of viewers saw the black and gold hand logo in use by a group of young and attractive television characters portraying lifeguards in all types of heroic adventures. The conscious and subconscious linking of Body Glove to the on-screen active lifestyle and heroics left a favorable and lasting impression of the brand.

As the company met with potential business partners in US and international markets, questions about *Baywatch* almost always came up. The program's portrayal of the Southern California lifestyle, and Body Glove as the brand that most represented it, added to Body Glove's cool image worldwide.

Because of the cold Pacific Ocean, stars who had any water scenes wanted Body Glove wetsuits. Jack LaLanne wore Dive N' Surf and Body Glove wetsuits in his cold-water stunts where he towed boats, loaded with people, for great distances, often swimming in very cold water and against strong currents.

While filming *Overboard*, Goldie Hawn and Kurt Russell wore Body Glove nude wetsuits under their clothes to brave the cold water they had to jump into. Robert De

Magazine spread with David Hasselhoff, Erika Eleniak and young actor in Body Glove wetsuits. Photo credit: Body Glove International

Niro and Charles Grodin wore them in the movie *Midnight Run*. The nude suits were quite popular at the time because they allowed the actors to wear their normal attire and viewers could not tell that they were in wetsuits.

Over many years, Body Glove has supplied one of the most successful major movie franchises, *James Bond*, with wetsuits for Sean Connery, Timothy Dalton, and Pierce Brosnan.

The "Frenchie" wetsuit worn by Heather Locklear, Heather Thomas, and Rachel Hunter led to the start of Body Glove swimwear. In 1992, Rachel Hunter went to Catalina Island on the *Disappearance* with Bob Meistrell for a fashion catalog shoot. She took her film crew and *Entertainment Tonight* staff. Bob remembered taking Rod Stewart out diving while Rod's wife Rachel and the photographer Kal Yee got to work on the catalog.

Randy Meistrell remembers making a neoprene sweater for actor Robert Englund, who starred as Freddy Krueger in *A Nightmare on Elm Street* and its sequels, to match that evil character's black-and-red-striped attire that he wore in his movies.

The recognition of Body Glove as the premiere surf brand led to more and more interest by the Hollywood movie industry. When Hollywood finally decided in 1987 to make a surf movie, *North Shore*, there was no other option but to go with Body Glove. Little did the company know then that pro surfer Scott Daley, who had a spot in *North Shore*, would become Body Glove's vice president of marketing some years later.

In the early 1950s, a man named Jack Russell often hung around Dive N' Surf. He always wore a jumpsuit that zipped up the front. Bev Morgan's daughter Connie remembers being in the shop when she was little, and he would come in all the time. Rusell would always talk to Bill and Bob and Bev about how he wanted to rob Las

Vegas and how he had a plan. The guys laughed him off and Bev told him, "Instead of actually doing it, why don't you write it down?" One day Russell asked to borrow Bev's truck, and Bev reluctantly gave in. About twenty minutes later, the police called Bev and said that a truck registered to his name was parked in the middle of an intersection, keys in the ignition, motor running. Bev went and retrieved the truck and, given that Russell was kind of a quirky guy, never thought much of it.

Russell disappeared for a while, eventually showing up with a published book titled *Ocean's 11*. Frank Sinatra purchased the rights to make it into a motion picture and used his group of pals, the "Rat Pack," to star in it. Laughing, Bev Morgan said, "In the mix of people and activities at that time were Jack Russell, Frank Sinatra, *Ocean's 11*, the Meistrells, *Sea Hunt*, and the rest of the usual suspects."

For almost sixty years, Body Glove and Hollywood have been linked in cinema and television, and the future looks just as bright.

11

THE *EMERALD*—
BILL AND BOB
BECOME SALVORS

On June 7, 1963, Frank Wynn was at the helm of *Emerald*, his 55-foot yawl, returning to Redondo Beach Marina from a day at Catalina Island, when he realized a heavy following sea was pushing him directly into the breakwater. He immediately lowered his sails and started his engine, which sputtered and died. *Emerald* struck the rocks and sank in four minutes. Wynn, his wife and daughter, plus two friends went into the water with life jackets, while his dog scrambled onto the breakwater's rocks. People who saw the sinking called the Harbor Patrol, and the responding crew pulled Wynn and the others aboard the *Baywatch II*.

Emerald *prior to its sinking.*
Photo credit: Don Siverts

Leonard Wibberley, a resident of Hermosa Beach, was the author of *The Mouse That Roared* and *The Mouse on the Moon*, and more than a hundred other titles. He was an amateur diver who met Bill and Bob at Dive N' Surf and often dove with them and the other divers who hung out at the shop.

Wibberley heard about the sinking and went to the salvage auction arranged by the boat's insurance company, which was anxious to sell because Emerald was a hazard to navigation. Plus, it estimated the salvage costs would be at least $20,000.

Wibberley, not being an expert in boat salvaging, found this to be a great plot for a book he would later publish, *The Raising of the Dubhe* (as Patrick O'Connor). Wibberley, Bill and Bob, and their friend Don Siverts, all amateur salvagers, paid just $500 at auction for the boat, which sat in 50 feet of water. Wibberley made the three men partners in the project to raise the *Emerald*. Initially, they thought they would raise her to sell off any parts worth the effort but, once they dove down and saw she was in pretty good condition, they decided to bring her up for restoration.

Bill and Bob wanted to ensure that when they raised the sailboat it would not crash against the breakwater again. So they separated the boat's two anchors from their chains, tied lines to them, and walked them out along the bottom to where the anchors would dig in and have enough line to hold the boat in place. Connecting the ends of the lines to the sheet windlasses on the boat, they cranked in the lines until they were taut.

Bill, Bob, and Don, all experienced skin divers, decided to use a diver's solution thought up by Bill: "Let's hang inner tubes on her and fill them with air from scuba tanks." They had considered using ping pong balls and other ideas, but Bill's suggestion of inner tubes seemed the best.

So they bought 140 inner tubes and spent three days diving on the boat. They made a bridle of the anchor chain, to which they attached inner tubes. They connected the tubes to the boat's winches and steering wheel and all along the outside of the deck. Using air from additional scuba tanks, they filled each of the inner tubes.

Realizing they needed a way to communicate underwater, they devised a plan to make a washtub their communications center. Bill and Bob took their mother's recent-

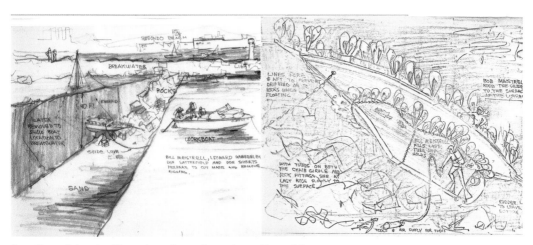

Don Siverts' sketch of how they planned to salvage Emerald.
Photo credit: Don Siverts

Sketch by Don Siverts of how they cut off the mast
underwater.
Photo credit: Don Siverts

ly bought washtub, drilled four holes on the edges, and chained it to the deck of the sunken boat. After they used their regulators to fill the upside-down tub with air, it lifted off of the deck and floated upside down, suspended. They swam into the tub, removed their mouthpieces, and while breathing the trapped air, discussed their next steps in the boat's recovery.

Local reporters and residents watching the operation asked Leonard Wibberley when he thought the boat would be salvaged. Without hesitation he pronounced that the boat would be up "At noon on Tuesday." Skeptics laughed at Wibberley's brazen statement.

As they were filling the 140th tube, the vessel started to lift. Very slowly, with Bill and Bob sitting on the deck, the boat lifted off the bottom and rose to the surface. The people gathered on the nearby breakwater laughed loudly when they heard Bill and Bob joke about being the only two captains they knew who had come up with the ship rather than going down with the ship. Then someone in the assembled crowd realized that the time was exactly noon, Tuesday, June 11.

Emerald was towed and anchored inside the breakwater, where Bill and Bob began to repair the holes in its hull. When it was safe to move, they had it towed to a shipyard in San Pedro where the repairs continued. All together, the men spent about $12,000. In return, they had a handsome sailing yawl that had been insured for $50,000.

Emerald *with attached tubes after being towed into the harbor.*
Photo credit: Don Siverts

Pumping water out of Emerald *at a slip in the harbor.*
Photo credit: Don Siverts

Green Light Turned On For Gemini

WASHINGTON (UPI)—Space Chief James E. Webb today closed the door on any more Mercury space shots.

The next U.S. manned space flight, possibly 16 months off, will be a two-man shot to inaugurate Project Gemini.

Webb, head of the National Aeronautics and Space Administration (NASA), formally signaled the end of the Mercury program in testimony before the Senate Space Committee.

Pleas Rejected

In effect rejecting pleas by Mercury astronauts and some others for one more single - man flight, Webb said NASA would now concentrate on Project Gemini, the second phase of its long-range program to send an American to the moon.

Gemini envisions putting two men in orbit in the same vehicle for extended periods—possibly as long as two weeks. But the program—the forerunner to moon-landing Project Apollo—is running behind schedule and the first shot could be 16 months away.

NASA Request

However, in testifying on NASA's request for a $5.7 billion appropriation, Webb said finally: "There will be no further Mercury shots. We will concentrate

(Continued on Page 2, Col. 3)

Searchers On Trail Of Escapees

FLORENCE, Ariz. (UPI)—Hundreds of searchers pressed hard on the heels of five desperate, armed prison escapes today after capturing two.

The seven used smuggled guns to disarm guards and flee from a work party Tuesday afternoon. The convicts included two mur-

Leader In NAACP Shot Down

JACKSON, Miss. (UPI)— Civil rights strategist Medgar Evers, who once vowed to remain in Mississippi "even if it means making the ultimate sacrifice," was shot to death by a sniper early today.

Evers, 37, fell in the driveway of his modest home with a bullet in his back and died about 15 minutes later at the University of Mississippi Medical Center. En route to the hospital, he yelled several times: "Turn me loose," then lapsed into unconsciousness.

Jackson Mayor Allen Thompson interrupted a Florida vacation to return to the Mississippi capital, plagued in recent weeks by civil rights protests, and ordered local police to put all their resources into an investigation of Evers' death.

In Washington, the FBI offered its full laboratory and identification facilities to the local investigators.

It was the third death in the South in the past two months involving participants in racial activities.

Baltimore postman William L.

NIGHT FINAL **Daily Breeze**

69th Year—No. 163   Wednesday, June 12, 1963   96 88 Pages Today

SALVAGE DIVERS—Clamber across the deck of the Emerald, 50-foot sail boat riding just beneath the surface and supported by 250 air-filled inner tubes. The Emerald sank Friday afternoon when it foundered on Redondo Beach King Harbor Breakwater rocks. It was raised yesterday by four persons, including co-owners of Dive N' Surf sporting goods, Redondo, who purchased salvage rights for $500. The craft was valued at $53,000.
(Daily Breeze photo)

'OOOPS, SHE'S AFLOAT'

Yawl Salvage Success Came Almost by Surprise

Plenty of ingenuity and sweat was needed to raise the sunken yawl hulk, Emerald.

The Emerald smashed last Friday against Redondo Beach King Harbor rocks and sank in 40 feet of water.

Yesterday, five skindivers using 250 air-filled inner tubes raised the 53-foot Emerald, which was

experts told him, and the other three co-salvagers, the Emerald could never be raised.

'It'll Break Up'

"It'll break up, if you try to bring it to the surface," the experts told the South Bay salvagers, who purchased salvage rights from an insurance company for

Meistrell said four divers worked in shifts filling the tubes.

He said he and another diver were attaching tubes to the stern section, when they found the boat was brought to the surface.

"We didn't even know we were
(Continued on Page 2, Col. 6)

Greek King Will Seek Crisis Help

ATHENS, Greece (AP)—King Paul opened a round of consultations today designed to bring Greece out of its first real government crisis in seven years.

The monarch conferred with Constantine Rodopoulos, president of Parliament, and then invited two leading opponents of Constantine Caramanlis to a palace conference.

Emerald's *restoration process.*
Photo credit: Don Siverts

After this initial success, Bill and Bob sought other opportunities to use their diving skills and adventurous natures to find and salvage other wrecks. Because of the publicity surrounding the *Emerald's* recovery, they became known as "salvage experts." Soon they were called by an insurance company to salvage a 30-foot sailboat that had sunk off San Pedro.

They bought twenty-five inner tubes and tied them to the boat before leaving to get food and buy some additional tubes. When they got back to the site, and before they could dive again, they ran into the boat's owner, the insurance agent, and the adjuster. The in-

Bill and Bob working on the Emerald.
Photo credit: Don Siverts

surance agent asked, "When is it coming up?" They said, "Right now!" Grabbing the bow and stern lines, they pulled up, and to the surprise of Bill and Bob the boat rose quickly to the surface right in front of everyone. That got a good laugh and a big smile from the boat's owner.

The last salvage event involved not boats but aircraft. On January 13, 1969, Scandinavian Airlines System Flight 933, with nine crew members and thirty-six passengers, crashed into Santa Monica Bay about six miles from Los Angeles International Airport, its intended destination. In addition to a US Coast Guard boat, a Los Angeles County Baywatch rescue craft was dispatched to the scene. Many small boat operators also responded. Thirty people survived and fifteen died.

The four-jet DC-8 broke into three pieces, with one large part of the fuselage remaining afloat. The next day the Meistrells were engaged to tow the floating portion of the aircraft to shore. Using the *Que Paso*, they slowly and carefully pulled the wreckage until it sank in about 100 feet of water near shore. Although the Meistrells offered to raise the fuselage using their previously successful inner tube method, the authorities decided to use two barges.

Overall, Bill and Bob recovered one aircraft and five boats, including one off Palos Verdes and one inside the Redondo Beach breakwater. In an interesting twist of fate, the money they made from the sale of the Emerald soon would pay for one of their other boyhood dreams—owning a submarine.

How the Que Paso *was named: A friend rang on Bill's door and when Bill answered it the guy said "Que Paso?" Bill asked what that meant and the guy said "What's Happening?" On the spot, Bill decided to name the boat that.*

Jackie Meistrell (left) and Patty Meistrell christen the Que Paso *with a bottle of champagne.*
Photo credit: Meistrell Archive

Bill, Bob and friends on their first trip on the Que Paso.
Photo credit: Meistrell Archive

12

CARDBOARD BOXES TO MINI-SUBS

With the first of Bill and Bob's childhood objectives—to be deep-sea divers—now a reality, they didn't waste a lot of time moving on toward their second objective—to own a submarine.

Back in Missouri they had made cardboard "submarines" out of the boxes refrigerators and stoves came in when delivered to their brother's appliance store. These large cartons, with "portholes" cut out of the sides and a "periscope" made from a cardboard tube attached to the top, the boys had a perfectly fun submarine for all the neighborhood kids to enjoy. While their mother didn't like the mushy cardboard mess that resulted when it rained on the subs, she tolerated it because she knew how much Bill and Bob loved their fantasy world of undersea adventure.

Years later, when Bill and Bob turned their talents to creating a real

Bob (left) and Bill accomplished their dream and were proud owners of their first submarine. Photo credit: Meistrell Archive

submarine, they did it the same way they did everything else—with great enthusiasm. When Don Siverts went to work at Dive N' Surf, he told Bill and Bob he wanted to build a submarine, which Bob recalled was one of the reasons they hired him.

Siverts, however, wanted to build a submarine that would crawl along the bottom, while Bob wanted one that would "fly" through the water. After the *Emerald* had been restored, Bill and Bob sold it to Don Siverts, but they hadn't been paid for it yet. They weren't worried because they knew Don would come through in the end, and he did.

When Don eventually sold the *Emerald*, Bob told him to keep the money, rather than paying them, and invest it in the building of a sub. So Bill, Bob, and Don started a dive company, Undersea Graphics, and began the construction of a submarine, which they would use in underwater inspections, and adventures.

With Don's usual vigor, he immediately converted his garage into a submarine manufacturing plant, or at least a smaller version of that. In no time at all, pipes, valves, and various parts

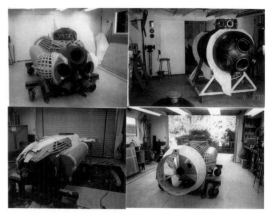

Don Siverts' garage with the structure of the submarine model made of wood.
Photo credit: Don Siverts

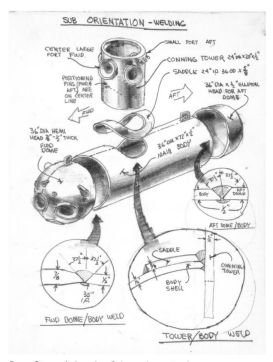

Don Siverts' sketch of the submarine's components.
Photo credit: Don Siverts

started to arrive at Don's garage, and the sub soon came to life. Don designed a two-man sub, which pleased Bob because he didn't want to dive by himself.

They tested the sub, appropriately named *Snooper,* in the waters around Redondo Beach, and then decided to take it to Catalina Island. Using the power cruiser *Que Paso,* which they bought after the sale of the Emerald, they transported the sub the twenty-six miles to Cherry Cove, one of their favorite diving spots. When they got there they learned that a diver had died off Ship Rock and was on the bottom, 178 feet below.

No one had been able to recover the diver's body, so Bob and Don offered to use the sub. They took *Snooper* down and looked all around Ship Rock, and Bob saw the body. Don maneuvered the sub near the diver and used the sub's extendable arm to grasp his body, which they took to the surface and turned over to the authorities. They

Bill and son Billy at Catalina getting ready to launch Snooper.
Photo credit: Meistrell Archive

also recovered the man's watch and compass on a second dive. The sub's value quickly became apparent to the authorities and to the deceased man's family, all of whom were appreciative of Bob and Don's help.

They took the sub down for a third time that day in another area, this time to a depth of 535 feet, before moving to Bird Rock, where they rose toward the surface. Just as they were about to end the dive, and at a depth of 250 feet, they saw a cave and ventured up to it for a closer look, a little too close. Bob and Don had the sickening realization that they had become stuck in the mouth of the cave. No matter what they did, the sub would not budge.

They radioed to the *Que Paso* that they were stuck, and Bill and a friend prepared to make an emergency dive with the triple tanks and dual regulator configuration they had used on their inspections for the power company. Bob and Don rocked the sub to try to free it from the cave, but because *Snooper* did not have a direct reverse, they had to turn the motor to one side and then the other to inch them back and forth in order to get the sub to move.

Gradually they freed the sub from the cave, and they radioed up to Bill to tell him not to dive. That day the total time Bob and Don spent underwater was five and a half hours, during which they recovered a dead diver, dove to a depth of 535 feet, and got stuck in a cave. Not bad for their first real test of their first submarine. The most interesting part is that Bob and Don never feared being stuck; if they panicked at all, Bob said, "We panicked quietly." They knew that if they really got into trouble, the divers on the boat would come down and save them. Bob re-

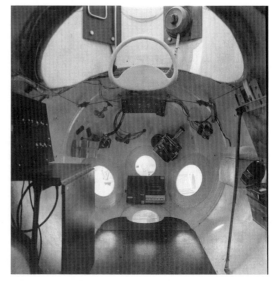

View of the inside of Snooper.
Photo credit: Don Siverts

called that it felt a little crowded in there after so long underwater, but he laughed when he told the story, and one could see that, even after all the intervening years, he still got excited about the adventures.

They were great dives Donald C. Siverts

Don Siverts and Bob in front of the submarine.
Photo credit: Don Siverts

13

KEEP YOUR OCEAN BLUE

During the successful rise of Body Glove to the top of the surfing and diving worlds, Bill and Bob made an early commitment to protect nature, give back to the industries they loved, and provide education to young people about the importance of living life to the fullest and being responsible for one's actions.

Their passion for the ocean led Bill and Bob to fight for clean oceans and protected species. In the 1960s, before the word "ecology" became a buzzword, Bill and Bob pioneered the environmental movement with a homegrown effort in Redondo Beach they called "Keep Your Ocean Blue." Body Glove made and distributed thousands of bumper stickers with "Keep Your Ocean Blue" on them.

Body Glove's logo for the "Keep Your Ocean Blue" campaign.
Photo credit: Body Glove International

Bob (left) and Bill getting ready for a harbor clean up dive.
Photo credit: Meistrell Archive

In the early 1960s Bob organized the first cleanup dive in Redondo's King Harbor. Recognizing that a lot of trash had sunk to the bottom of the marina, he tried to arrange an underwater cleanup whereby scuba divers he knew would dive the harbor and collect the debris. To his surprise, the city balked at this idea because it was afraid the divers would be injured, or worse, and the city would be sued. Never one to let obstacles stand in his way for long, Bob called the city attorney and told him that he was going to write a letter to the *Daily Breeze*, the local newspaper, to tell everyone that the city didn't want to clean up the marina. He got approval right away, and the underwater environment was cleaned up.

Even though the twins were focused on business, they always were looking for ways to protect the environment, especially in disastrous situations. On March 24, 1989, the single-hull tanker Exxon Valdez ran aground on Bligh Reef in Prince William Sound, near Valdez, Alaska. Approximately 270,000 barrels of crude oil spilled into the Sound and neighboring Gulf of Alaska. According to the *Dictionary of American History* and numerous other sources, the oil spill killed "an estimated 250,000 seabirds, 2,800 sea otters, 300 harbor seals, 150 bald eagles, up to 22 killer whales, and billions of salmon and herring eggs."

A friend of Bill's came to him with an idea to use bird feathers, which are extremely absorbent, to pick up the oil. Bill designed a tube-shaped potato sack that could be stuffed with feathers and put into the water to absorb the oil. He patented the device, which he called the "Oil Glove."

Bill also invented a machine that would blow the feathers into the tubes so they wouldn't have to be filled by hand. During that time, the Body Glove factory turned into a wetsuit-manufacturing space *and* a feathery mess. Feathers flew everywhere in the manufacturing plant, and wetsuit production practically came to a halt until the team could figure out a better process.

Bill flew to Alaska and filmed a demonstration of how the Oil Glove worked. He sent video cassettes along with written material to Alaska's US senators and representatives. It soon became obvious, however, that the authorities were not interested in a creative and innovative solution to the problem. Body Glove lost the $50,000 it had invested, but at least Bill and Bob knew that they had tried to provide real and effective assistance.

Bill and Bob and their families loved to dive off the coast of Catalina Island, where giant California black sea bass often are found. These 300–400 pound fish are gentle and inquisitive, often swimming close to divers.

On June 12, 2001, California Department of Fish and Game officers discovered a 350-pound sea bass with a spear stuck in its body, and others with gashes and nicks on their scales that some believe resulted from attacks by spear fishermen. That's why Bob offered a $5,000 reward for information leading to the arrest and conviction of anyone who kills a giant sea bass in California. Bob's offer came immediately after California passed a law prohibiting fishing for giant sea bass, which can grow to 6 feet and 400 pounds.

Both Bill and Bob served the South Bay community in a variety of positions to protect the ocean and its inhabitants, preserve the coastal shores, and expand public awareness about these important assets. Just one example of their influence was Bob's role on the board of the Catalina Island Conservancy Divers, a group he co-founded. The group's projects measured water temperatures and currents around the island, created an abalone program that

Bill in Alaska testing the Oil Glove soaked in oil.
Photo credit: Body Glove International

South Bay Business

Local designs glove to sop up oil spills

by Robin Kemp

It's not every day that a disaster of the magnitude of the Exxon oil spill in Alaska's Prince William Sound can provide both the glint of gold and a glimmer of hope.

Inventor Bill Lafay and Body Glove owner Bill Meistrell have created the Oil Glove, the major operating principle of which is common sense. As Lafay watched the news of the spill a few weeks ago, he saw that all-too-familiar electronic image of a pathetic, oil-coated bird, dying from the weight of the oil that stuck stubbornly to its feathers.

Suddenly, it occurred to him: nothing soaks up oil faster than waterfowl. Or more specifically, feathers.

Lafay designed a packet of duck feathers contained by polypropylene mesh, to be tossed onto the slick, and showed it to Meistrell at Body Glove.

"He just brought some small prototypes," said Meistrell. The pair named the thing 'Oil Glove' and applied for a patent. On April 15, they went to Smith Island in Prince William Sound to videotape their prototype test.

Seeing is believing. Dressed in an orange cleanup suit and slipping on the oil-coated rocks, Lafay explained the experiment as it progressed. He expected the Oil Glove to pick up between 15 and 30 times its weight in oil.

Lafay waded into the water and dropped his prototype onto the slick. He turned it over a few times. The pad of white feathers grew brownish-black within a minute. When Lafay lifted the Oil Glove, clear water ran off of it, back into the sea. The oil stuck.

Lafay waddled and waded back to shore, and weighed the prototype on a kitchen scale. It weighed eight pounds -- 32 times its dry weight.

Hey, wait a minute, some cynics have said. Just how much of that extra weight is water?

Think about it, said Lafay. Duck feathers repel water. So does oil. The water ran off. The oil stuck.

"It's on Exxon's desk and they're looking at it," said Lafay. The urgency in his voice tumbles out. "In about a month, all the waterfowl of America will arrive in Prince William Sound. Either I'm gonna clean it up, or one million geese are gonna do it for them."

Who's looking at the prototype at Exxon? "They keep bringing in a new guy about every two weeks, no kidding," Meistrell laughed sardonically. "They just point the finger, 'Talk to him,'

'Talk to that one.' Nobody's in charge of making big decisions."

Meistrell is frustrated with the cleanup bureaucracy. "Nobody's in control," he said. "Exxon wants the government to clean up the spill. Everyone's so concerned with washing the beach off. The beaches there are done. Killed. You can't save them. What they should be working on is the oil in the water."

Both Lafay and Meistrell pointed out the ineffectiveness of the beach cleanup. "They need *help*," Lafay said. "This little town of Homer, these people are cutting logs down and nailing plywood to them to try to keep the oil off their beaches." When the Environmental Protection Agency finally agreed to test the Oil Glove, Lafay said, the cleanup crews used it to rub the rocks on the beach.

"They had it all wrong," Lafay said. "It's designed to soak up oil on the surface of the water. You've gotta get it up out of the water.

"You can clean up the beach, and it'll look great, but around the corner is the slick. One tide change, one wind change, and it'll come right back."

Meistrell added, "They're going to put 4,000 people on the beach cleaning rocks. They have no idea how to deal with this."

Representatives from the governors' offices in Alaska and Florida and the mayor of Valdez

have expressed support for the invention, according to Lafay. He added that he would like to seek the Sierra Club's endorsement.

Jeff Widen, spokesman for the Sierra Club's Southern California office, said that while the group doesn't actually endorse products, they do support or oppose processes.

Although the organization has not yet considered the Oil Glove, Widen said, "This is something we would potentially take a position on. It's not the simplest process in the world. If he is seeking Sierra Club support, I could in some way get him to talk to the right folks."

Meanwhile, the damage spreads. Lafay has returned to Alaska to get somebody—anybody—to start using the Oil Glove. "We could give them all we could make if they would use it," Meistrell said. "We don't care if we get paid for it or not. Of course, it would be nice if we could eventually get our investment back."

If the Oil Glove catches on, the potential profit is staggering. But the pair said money is not the motivating factor.

"A one-pound bird picks up about 35 pounds of oil," Meistrell said. "I picked up a cormorant, and it weighed about 30 pounds. That's a pretty small bird." The pair have vowed to return to Alaska in May to begin their own cleanup. *ER*

Article written in a South Bay business section
about the Oil Glove design.
Photo credit: Meistrell Archive

planted approximately eighteen thousand abalone from the Body Glove dive boat, and conducted a kelp restoration program.

Another community effort is Body Glove's donation of three-hour boat rides on the *Disappearance*, its 72-foot dive boat, as auction items for different charities, including the Wounded Warrior Project, the American Cancer Society, the Switzer Learning Center, and a host of other worthwhile organizations. Each year Body Glove donated about fifty trips on the boat.

In 2005 Bob noticed that floating bottles, cans, plastic, and other trash accumulated in the corners of the marina. He bought trash cans and pool nets with long poles, which he attached to the cans so they could be used to pick up the debris. Altogether, he put twelve cans in place, and he encouraged residents of King Harbor to use them to keep their marina clean. Bob even went around and collected the trash bags from the cans until the job got taken over by others.

Bob placed a newspaper ad to bring awareness that Black Sea Bass was a protected species.
Photo credit: Meistrell Archive

One of the trash cans Bob placed on every dock in Redondo's King Harbor and some of the trash that was collected.
Photo credit: Body Glove International

14

TREASURE HUNTING BECOMES A REALITY

With the success of their diving business and the initial trials of their new submarine, Bill and Bob had achieved two of their boyhood dreams. Now, with the new experience of salvaging boats, they were ready to pursue their third objective—hunting for underwater treasure.

Bill and Bob were introduced to treasure diving by Dick Anderson, an experienced local commercial diver who had recovered part of the gold treasure from the *Maravilla (Nuestra Señora de las Maravillas),* a Spanish galleon that sank in 1656 near Grand Bahama Island. Anderson partnered with treasure hunter Robert Marx, who had searched for the *Maravilla* for more than twelve years before discovering her remains in 1972.

Marx had recovered gold and artifacts worth millions, but lost it all to the Bahamian government when he entered port and was met by armed guards and a newly elected Prime Minister who rejected earlier deals with Marx. All of the treasure was seized, and Marx was expelled from the country and banned from returning to the Bahamas.

With Marx unable to return, Dick Anderson, who knew the ship's location, organized a treasure hunt in 1980, with Bill and Bob investing in the project. Composed of local investors, divers, and adventurers, the team of treasure hunters departed Santa Barbara, California, on the *Coral Sea,* a dive boat outfitted for the long journey. Bill and Bob each put up $10,000, the going rate for a 1 percent share of any treasure they

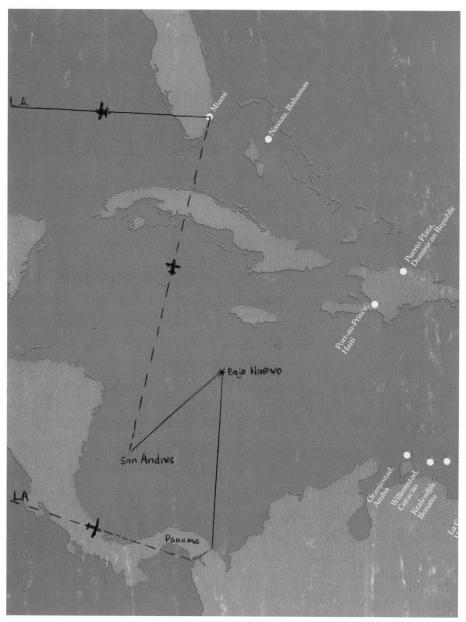

Map of their trip through the Panama Canal and Caribbean.
Photo credit: Joe Meistrell

The group aboard the vessel. Bill is fifth from right.
Photo credit: Joe Meistrell

Caption: Bill on the treasure hunt.
Photo credit: Joe Meistrell

might discover. When the *Coral Sea* set sail, Bill, his older brother Joe, and Joe's son, called Lil Joe, were on board.

The vessel made it down the west coast and through the Panama Canal into the Caribbean Sea, where things got dicey. While in Colombian waters, the *Coral Sea* was boarded by Colombian navy personnel and placed under arrest on a charge of smuggling guns to Nicaragua. Their passports were seized, and for a full week, the would-be treasure hunters were held aboard the *Coral Sea*. They were released by the guards, whom they had befriended, when the Colombians could find no evidence.

Allowed to continue their journey, the crew soon arrived at the *Maravilla's* supposed site, known only to Robert Marx and Dick Anderson. Diving operations began at once and, despite centuries of shifting sands and the natural growth of white coral, discoveries came to the surface: emeralds, pieces of eight, amethysts, silver bars, and a variety of artifacts, such as guns, swords, and other parts of the ship. But the main cargo hold, which had broken off from the bow portion Marx had found previously, was not located.

The Coral Sea *with large sand blasting tube at the stern.*
Photo credit: Joe Meistrell

The crew returned home and the investors were paid off, with everyone earning about the same amount they had invested.

Bill and Bob's next treasure hunt was an investment in an expedition to Cocos Island, some 375 miles off the Pacific Coast of Costa Rica. Actually, they invested in two trips to Cocos Island, but they had the same result as every other treasure hunter who has searched for the large cache of gold, silver, and jewels said to be buried there.

The British ship *Mary Deare*, engaged to transport the great wealth from churches in Lima, Peru, to Spain, was taken over by its mutinous crew, which headed directly for the uninhabited Cocos Island. After burying the treasure in a cave, the mutineers sailed

Some of the gold and silver that they found.
Photo credit: Joe Meistrell

More treasure from the shipwreck.
Photo credit: Joe Meistrell

to Panama, where all were arrested and executed except for three who promised to help authorities recover the treasure. Through a series of errors and misadventures, the three escaped and hid in the jungle, taking the treasure's location with them. The ensuing years have yet to reveal the treasure that Bill and Bob invested in, believed to be worth over $30 million in today's market.

Bill and Bob's fourth, and last, treasure hunt was very different from the first three. To begin with, it actually made them some money. Not much—but about $139,000 is far better than breaking even or losing their investments, as they did on the first three.

Another difference was that the expedition used the two-person submarine, *Snooper*, built earlier by Don Siverts and the Meistrells. Don and his son, Curt, transported the sub to San Francisco, where they teamed up with Deep Sea Research, Inc. (DSR), professional ship salvors, who had been searching for the *Brother Jonathan* for years. Under the command of Don Knight, DSR had its own mini-submarine, Delta, which had been used successfully in other treasure hunts. Don Siverts was added to the team because he and his Undersea Graphics company, created with the Meistrells for underwater work and photography, had an excellent reputation for underwater work with *Snooper*.

On July 30, 1865, the side-wheel steamer *Brother Jonathan* ran into a heavy gale just hours after leaving San Francisco harbor on its way north to Portland, Oregon, and Vancouver, Canada. The seas were so large near the California-Oregon border that the captain ordered the ship to come about and return to the harbor of Crescent City, California. Near the port the ship struck a huge rock, tearing a hole in its hull. Within five minutes, passengers and crew were ordered to abandon ship. Only a single lifeboat—with eleven crew members, five women, and three children on board—managed to escape the wreck and make it safely to Crescent City.

On the sunken vessel were crates of newly-minted $20 gold coins, including the annual treaty payments for Indian tribes, Wells Fargo shipments consigned for Portland and Vancouver, and gold and jewelry belonging to passengers. According to reports, the gold alone was valued at $50 million in today's dollars. Although ships and divers searched for the sunken treasure two weeks after the disaster, the ship's treasure of gold and artifacts remained one of the Pacific's greatest secrets for over 125 years.

At daybreak on October 1, 1993, Siverts and *Snooper* were lowered into the ocean from the mother ship. Don took Snooper down to the dark bottom, 250 feet below, where he began his search for the shipwreck. With outside lights on, he was able to see only 8 to 10 feet ahead, but what he saw interested him greatly.

Rockfish in increasingly large numbers swam around his sub and seemed to be leading off to his port side, so he steered in that direction. He knew from prior underwater work that large schools of fish often congregated in and around wrecks, so he followed the fish.

Slowly moving *Snooper* along the bottom through the murky water, Don saw ahead of him a darker object that contrasted with the ocean's grayness. It began to loom larger until, to his surprise, he recognized the shape of a paddlewheel and its connecting shaft, clear proof he had found the remains of the *Brother Jonathan*, the only paddle-wheeler to have sunk off this part of the California coast.

With the sub's camcorder capturing the scene as it unfolded, Don maneuvered carefully along the hull and radioed to the crew on the mother ship, "I've found the target. I think I've found the ship."

After Don returned to the safety of the mother ship, he and the crew viewed the videotape, and everyone yelled with excitement when they saw the shipwreck appearing out of the depths. Little did they know, however, that as difficult as finding the *Brother Jonathan* had been, keeping her treasures would be a much more difficult and costly task.

On March 15, 1995, after thousands of dollars had been spent on legal fees, Deep Sea Research won the court battle against the State of California, which had claimed the *Brother Jonathan*. Over the ensuing years, DSR successfully recovered some $5 million in gold coins and other treasures from the wreck. Don Siverts and the Meistrells earned about $139,000 for their efforts.

Although they never struck it rich through their treasure-hunting adventures, Bill and Bob fulfilled their third and final childhood dream. They were ready to move on to something new and exciting. That's when Ed Janss entered the scene.

15

DIVE ADVENTURES

hortly after creating its dive certification course, one of Dive N' Surf's students, Ed (Edwin) Janss, became very influential in Bill and Bob's lives by introducing them to the wide world of international travel and adventure. A California developer, Janss signed up for dive training and Bob became his instructor and friend.

One of the Galapagos Islands visited by Bob and his friends.
Photo credit: Meistrell Archive

Ed Janss knew several marine scientists who wanted to go to the Galapagos Islands to collect algae for research. Bob agreed to lead a twenty-one-day dive trip to the islands from Costa Rica. The trip went smoothly, with the scientists collecting algae and everyone enjoying the underwater beauty and the land excursions to see the diverse plants and animals.

On the last dive of the voyage, Bob suggested they dive a small island, and one of the local divers on board who knew Bill told them that it was infested with sharks. Bob said that's where they wanted to go, then, because they had been diving with hammerheads, white tips, and black tips every day.

This atoll was approachable from the ocean, so they maneuvered the dive boat inside the volcano and anchored. The next morning, wanting to dive on the edge of a 2,000-foot drop-off, Bob surveyed the water and saw sharks everywhere. He tied a blue fin and a black fin onto a line and threw it off the boat. If one of the fins came up with a shark bite, he would know he should wear the other color fin. As he pulled it back in, one of the divers asked what he was doing. Bob replied, "If they both come back in with teeth marks, I'm not going in the water!"

They waited a few hours, and as the baitfish disappeared, the current stopped and the sharks disappeared, Bob, Ed Janss, and Ed's wife Ann suited up and jumped in. They dove to 110 feet and didn't see a single shark, but Bob had a feeling something would happen on this trip.

The boat Bob and Ed Janss took to the Galapagos Islands.
Photo credit: Meistrell Archive

One of the giant iguanas in the Galapagos.
Photo credit: Meistrell Archive

Hammerhead and reef sharks that Bob and the group dove with in the Galapagos.
Photo credit: Meistrell Archive

Bob found a large rock in about 40 feet of water and sat on top of it, holding a speargun. About 5 feet below the surface, he had plenty of daylight and the visibility was crystal clear. As he looked around, he saw a large white shark approaching him. Here's how Bob described it:

I looked out and saw this monster swimming by. I yelled to Ed and pointed at the damned thing. Ed swam over to the rock and Ann slid under the rock's ledge. I just stayed there and the shark kept coming right at me. It was like a huge aircraft coming right at me. And he got right up to me and I just bent over backwards. His pectoral fins were like this [Bob held his arms out as wide as he could reach] and his dorsal fin was so large they could see it from the boat a long distance away. They thought it was a killer whale, so they came screaming over there.

Bob before a dive in the Galapagos.
Photo credit: Meistrell Archive

He just went right over me. About a 20-foot white shark. After he passed over me, I watched him and he came in again on me and the boat came in between him and me, and he just disappeared. The people on the boat measured him in comparison with the boat and confirmed he was 20 feet long.

People hearing this story often asked Bob if he panicked, and with his familiar smile and glint in his eye, he said, "You can't panic when your heart has stopped beating and you're not breathing."

One of the many fish species seen while diving the waters of the Galapagos.
Photo credit: Meistrell Archive

When Ed took friends on his boat, he always brought Bob along as a safety diver. On one trip, on their way down to Cabo San Lucas, Mexico, they anchored the boat in Magdalena Bay and decided

Bob wasn't the only twin to see a white shark. Bill and his family were at their mooring in Cherry Cove, Catalina Island, when a 17-foot white shark swam right next to the Que Paso.
Photo credit: Meistrell Archive

to go diving. The night before, Bob had read the book *Tales of the Sea*, and one of the stories was about a man who fell off a boat while traveling at night. No one heard him, and he became exhausted while treading water. As the story goes, an albatross landed next to him and allowed the man to hold its feet as it started flying, thus keeping him afloat.

The next morning, Bob and Ed Janss took their dinghy out to go diving. A man named Carlos drove the dinghy, and he was supposed to follow Bob and Ed's bubbles as they explored. When they got back to the surface, Carlos was too far away to see them. Just as they were beginning to get worried, a seagull landed on Bob's head, and Bob grabbed its feet. The gull tried to fly away, but Bob held onto him. The bird's flapping wings and screeches became his signaling device, and it wasn't long before Carlos spotted them and motored over to pick them up.

Gearing up for a morning dive in their Dive N' Surf Boston Whaler.
Photo credit: Meistrell Archive

Bob loved his trips with Ed Janss, but not all of Bob's adventures were to faraway or luxurious places. Bev Morgan said that when the twins started working at the shop, he would wake up at three in the morning and drive over to Bob's house in his truck. Because he didn't like to drive, he locked the passenger door and slid over, forcing Bob to drive. Then they continued to Bill's house, where they locked the passenger door again and slid over so Bill had to drive.

They would get down to the harbor, launch the boat, and be diving at

Getting some really big air off a wave in their Boston Whaler.
Photo credit: Meistrell Archive

Bill next to a plane they flew to the Sea of Cortez.
Photo credit: Meistrell Archive

Bill and a friend filling up tanks in Bahia de Los Angeles.
Photo credit: Meistrell Archive

the crack of dawn. When finished, they headed back to shore, close to the Redondo breakwater where Dive N' Surf was located. They steered the boat next to the wall, and one of them would hop up onto the rocks and run to open the shop, still in a dripping wetsuit. For Bill and Bob and their friends, those were the "good ole days."

Beside loving to go diving, they also loved to play jokes on each other. With Dive N' Surf still in its infancy, there were times when Bill, Bob, and Bev would sell everything they had in the store and then be out of inventory. At a surplus sale, they bought lockers, similar to gym lockers, with five or six doors. They each got a locker for their dive gear so they couldn't sell each other's gear when they were low on inventory. Well, Bill and Bob moved Bev's locker away from the wall and cut a hole in the back of it. There was a poster on the inside back of the locker, which covered up the hole.

Bev's gear kept disappearing, and he got really frustrated because he knew he had to use the lock to get into his locker, and neither Bill nor Bob had the combination to it. For about

six months, his gear sporadically disappeared and he had to order new gear.
Finally, Bev figured it out, but they had
him going for a long time.

Eventually, they were making
enough money to start exploring a little farther, this time in sea planes. Bev
and Bill had a friend who owned an airplane, and they flew down to the Mexican Baja Peninsula, where they landed
next to a hotel at *Bahia de Los Angeles*, a
small bay about halfway down the Baja
coast on the Sea of Cortez side of the
peninsula.

There was so much to see that they
would spend a week diving. The Sea of
Cortez had everything that California
had, such as sheepshead and black sea
bass, but it also had tropical fish, which
fascinated them. They would fly all of
their diving equipment down in the
airplane and have the locals take them
out in *pangas*, small flat-bottom boats
with outboard motors.

Another time, Bev and Bill rented
a seaplane called a Grumman Goose
that flew back and forth to Avalon on
Catalina Island. They loaded it up with
several divers and flew to San Nicolas
Island, the most remote of the Channel

Bill holding up his catch of the day after spearfishing in Mexico.
Photo credit: Meistrell Archive

Bev and Bill with local residents of Bahia de Los Angeles.
Photo credit: Meistrell Archive

Bob, Bev and Bill with their black sea bass.
Photo credit: Meistrell Archive

Islands off Ventura County, California. They landed the plane on the water, opened the
door, and inflated a life raft to go diving.

One of their most memorable trips was when Bill, Bob, and Bev drove down to
San Diego and launched their 16-foot boat with twin 35-horsepower Johnson motors.
They were off to the Coronado Islands in Mexican waters southwest of San Diego to
go spearfishing for black sea bass before they became illegal to hunt more than thirty
years later.

At the Coronados, Bev and Bill dived in, while Bob stayed at the boat's controls.
Bill was the first to spear a sea bass, which almost drowned him as it dragged him
through the ocean for twenty minutes before it tired enough for Bob (and Bev, who

had climbed back aboard) to catch up to him with the boat.

Bev and Bob soon jumped in, and Bev speared a large sea bass. He surfaced and yelled for the boat to approach. As he handed the line to Bill on the bow of the boat, Bev dropped his speargun. Before he dived to retrieve it, he saw Bill fall off the bow into the water as the fish jerked the line and proceeded to drag him, screaming and gasping, across the surface.

Bev and Bob climbed into the boat to give pursuit, and when they eventually caught up to the now very cold and tired Bill, they brought the monster fish onto the boat.

Bob, not to be outdone by his partners, jumped in and speared a sea bass in about 45 feet of water. With the first two fish, which weighed 383 and 391 pounds, secured in the small boat, they lashed Bob's 226-pound fish across the bow. Loaded with 1,000 pounds of fish and three men, the 16-foot boat sat low in the water as the spirited friends and partners headed back to San Diego.

Their black sea bass are taller than Bill, Bob and Bev.
Photo credit: Meistrell Archive

Bill later in life on the Body Glove dive boat
Disappearance *charting out the twins' next adventure.*
Photo credit: Meistrell Archive

Bob and Bev's fish were shared with family and friends, while Bill's sea bass was mounted and, to this day, hangs in the Body Glove conference room.

From the time Bill and Bob were kids, it was all about the adventure. That was something that stuck with them their entire lives. Jean-Michel Cousteau said, "I will always remember that when people asked my dad what he expected to find on the next expedition, his answer was always, 'If I knew, I would not go.' This is the same thing that the second-generation Meistrells say when they speak of Bill and Bob. That sometimes they went on an adventure just to go on an adventure and explore."

16

SECOND GENERATION TAKES NEOPRENE BEYOND THE WETSUIT

Bill and Bob enjoyed their lives and wanted their families to follow them into their business. In part because they didn't have a father, they felt strongly about giving their kids a chance to work with them in a family-owned-and-operated business.

The first of the second generation of Meistrells to join the company in a full-time paid position was Robbie, Bob's oldest son. After graduation from high school in 1970, Robbie set off with $400 and a surfboard to hit the surfing hot spots of Tahiti, New Zealand, Australia, and Hawaii. He described this trip as "the most significant event to change the way I looked at things."

After Robbie's stint running Blue Fin Aqua, a dive shop Bill and Bob owned in Inglewood, California, they offered him a chance to manage Dive N' Surf. With the knowledge he had gained at Blue Fin Aqua and from sales courses and management books, Robbie created and implemented an inventory control system, ordered all products, and worked on the sales floor two days a week. About a year later, he decided to enlarge the business. Robbie bought Zig Ziglar's audiotapes about selling, and he demanded that everyone go to Ziglar's high-energy seminars. Sales increased 10 to 15 percent immediately afterward.

(Left to Right) Ronnie, Bill, Billy, Robbie, Randy, and Bob in the South Bay just out of the water after a surf.
Photo credit: Body Glove International

Dive N' Surf continued to expand, with innovative sales and marketing ideas. All through the late 1970s and early 1980s, the company worked to maximize sales of all products. By 1983, Dive N' Surf's sales were well over $1 million per year, and in May, Robbie was elected president of the company and chairman of the board. He created annual business and management plans with very specific goals. The company was evolving into a more managed enterprise, which would be critical in the coming years.

(Left to right) Second generation Meistrells: Julie, Billy, Robbie, Ronnie, and Randy in the '80s.
Photo credit: Meistrell Archive

While Dive N' Surf remained a retail store in Redondo Beach, the second-generation Meistrells put their energy into the enhancement of the Body Glove brand. At this point, all five second-generation Meistrells were in the business. With Robbie focused on management, Billy Meistrell, Bill's son, was expanding the company's manufacturing capability by seeking international partners who could produce wetsuits. At the same time, Billy and Randy Meistrell, Bob's youngest son, were looking for other products that would both meet Body Glove standards and help strengthen their financial position. Julie, Bill's daughter, was in office administration, and Ronnie, Bob's middle son, was making sure Dive N' Surf was running smoothly.

Between 1983 and 1989, Body Glove sales worldwide increased significantly, making it one of the major players in water sports.

This transition from the first to the second generation running the business allowed Bill and Bob to continue their life of adventure. In 1982 Bill and Bob bought the boat of their dreams, the Disappearance. Originally owned by Ed Janss, this 72-foot Ditmar Donaldson custom-built yacht became the center of frequent family trips to Catalina Island and other favorite destinations.

Another key player entered the picture at this time. Russ Lesser, the current president of Body Glove International, first met Bill and Bob in 1962 when he and his brother, Rick, took scuba lessons from Bob. At the time, Russ was in college studying finance, and he told Bob that he wanted to become a certified public accountant. Bob told him that when he became an accountant, Bob would sign on Dive N' Surf as one of his clients. After graduation, Russ became a CPA and joined the accounting firm Windes and McClaughry, where he eventually became managing partner. Bob stayed true to his word, and Russ was hired to do Dive N' Surf's finances for twenty-five years before he became president of the company in 1990. From the moment Russ started working for the company, he became family, and that, no doubt, is a major reason why he has stayed with the company as accountant and president for forty-eight years.

(Left to right) Bob, Patty, Russ and Charlotte Lesser, and Bill.
Photo credit: Meistrell Archive

As Bill and Bob began to enjoy the fruits of their labors, the second generation took on the active management of Body Glove, each focusing on a different part of the business. After years of growing up and enjoying the active water sports lifestyle created by their fathers, it was time for the second generation to show their talents.

Because the second generation had shared in many of their fathers' adventures, they understood the importance of active lifestyles, especially around water. They surfed and dived and introduced their own children to these and other sports. They believed in and followed their fathers' mantra of "Love what you do, do what you love." And they continued the important conservation work begun years before by two men who understood that nature needed to be protected and preserved. As they made their own way in the family business, they each accepted and expanded on Bill and Bob's belief that customers must be treated with respect and honesty.

Under the management of Russ Lesser and the second-generation Meistrells, Body Glove expanded its product lines, markets, and international presence. The Body Glove hand logo became widely recognized throughout the United States and in major foreign countries as the brand best known for its quality and attractive water sports products.

Because there were few restrictions on imported goods, most other American wet-suit manufacturers had gone overseas for production, while Body Glove continued its US manufacturing. Soon, however, it became evident that to remain competitive in the US market, Body Glove would have to look to international manufacturing sources for its wetsuit and other product lines. Because the company had stringent employee safety standards in place, and paid better wages, it could not compete successfully against low-cost imports.

Body Glove found a high-quality manufacturer in Thailand to produce its classic wetsuits, the centerpiece of its product line. The company already had begun licensing other product categories, such as bathing suits and clothing, so it looked to license its wetsuit and water sports lines, also. As a result, Body Glove expanded into major US and several key foreign markets.

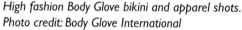

High fashion Body Glove bikini and apparel shots.
Photo credit: Body Glove International

One of the remarkable results of bringing the second generation of Meistrells into Body Glove was the development of new products entirely unrelated to diving and surfing. One such example was what Billy Meistrell achieved in the medical orthopedic market.

From the time he was six years old, Billy used to go to "work" with his father whenever he wasn't in school or doing other childhood things. He loved the time they spent together and learned much about the crafting of wetsuits. It was during these hours with Bill Meistrell that Billy developed his interest in making things and creating new products.

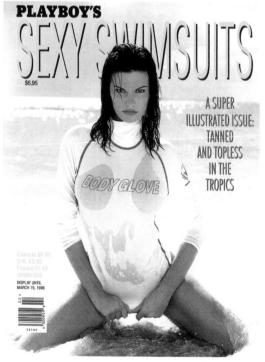

A model in Body Glove lycra on the cover of Playboy magazine.
Photo credit: Playboy magazine

Billy Meistrell working in the factory marking patterns to cut wetsuits.
Photo credit: Meistrell Archive

Billy led Body Glove into manufacturing neoprene products designed for professional and amateur athletes. In the late '70s he began working with Garrett Giemont, who at the time was the strength coach for the Los Angeles Rams professional football team. This was the perfect alliance to develop a line of orthopedic wear. After working with Giemont, Billy recognized that an entirely new market potential existed that had nothing to do with surfing or diving but yet focused on neoprene, the material from which Body Glove wetsuits were made.

Through his friendship with National Basketball Association star Kurt Rambis of the Los Angeles Lakers, Billy learned that Rambis had to ice down his knees multiple times a day. It was such a hassle making the ice bags and trying to Ace-bandage them

BODY GLOVE®

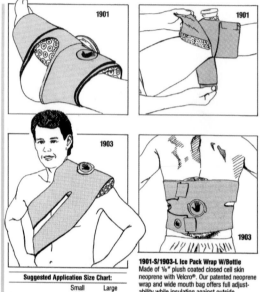

*B*ack in 1953 twin brothers Bob and Bill Meistrell began Dive N' Surf, Inc., recognized today as one of the oldest and most respected dive shops in the United States. It was during this period that the first Body Glove wet suit was constructed.

Since that time, Body Glove has expanded in size and scope. A new generation has led Body Glove into new ventures, including orthopedics, fashion and functional swimwear and clothing. Yet the Body Glove promise remains the same. We stand behind our products 100%.

Our pride and hard work has earned us a respected reputation for quality products and service around the world. Our highly trained staff uses only the finest materials available, while prompt delivery and competitive pricing have become trademarks.

Body Glove is constantly searching for ways in which to improve our products. Our research and development team is the best in the business, with total freedom to experiment. As a result, a wide variety of sizes, styles, and colors are always available to insure total satisfaction. In this way, tomorrow's needs are satisfied today.

From the entire Meistrell family, many thanks for considering Body Glove. We are proud to serve you, because Body Glove is everything your body would want it to be.

The Meistrells

Suggested Application Size Chart:

	Small 1901	Large 1903
Wrist	✓	✓
Elbow	✓	✓
Shoulders		✓
Neck		✓
Back		✓
Hips		✓
Thigh		✓
Knee	✓	✓
Ankle	✓	✓
Foot	✓	✓

1901-S/1903-L Ice Pack Wrap W/Bottle
Made of ⅛" plush coated closed cell skin neoprene with Velcro®. Our patented neoprene wrap and wide mouth bag offers full adjustability while insulating against outside temperature. It provides controlled pressure while it conforms to ankles, knees, elbows, shoulders, backs, etc. The first truly mobile hot or cold therapy product. Developed by Body Glove for immediate care of acute sports injuries. U.S. Patent No. 4585003.

Also available:

1901-AS Small and 1903-AL Large Ice Pack Wrap Without Bottle

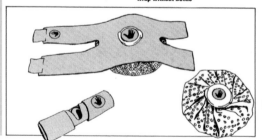

Page from Body Glove's orthopedic catalog.
Photo credit: Body Glove International

to his knees. After practice sessions or games, Kurt wrapped his knees, and then sat awaiting the inevitable pain that followed.

Visiting Kurt at his home one evening, and seeing the pain he was in and how involved he was with wrapping his knees to keep ice on the areas, Billy decided to invent a special knee wrap for him. After working through the night, he created a neoprene knee wrap with a built-in ice pack.

The next day, Billy gave the Body Glove knee wrap to Kurt to try out and, after putting ice in the pack and easily attaching the wrap to his knee with a self-adjusting Velcro material, Kurt was ecstatic. The knee wrap was simple, easy to put on and take off, and fit exactly where he needed it. Kurt asked Billy if he could make another for his other knee and several more for his teammates. Body Glove now had a new product that could reach every sports team, from high school to the professional leagues.

Billy also began working with the Lakers' athletic trainer, Gary Vitti, and with Pete Demers, trainer for the Los Angeles Kings professional hockey team. Teams playing the Lakers saw the innovative wraps that Kurt Rambis and Magic Johnson were wearing, both on and off the court, and Vitti and Demers introduced Billy to other trainers in the sports world.

This product was so unique that it received US Patent Number 4,585,003 on April 29th, 1986. Body Glove's neoprene wraps with built-in ice packs became extremely popular because combining the plush neoprene material with the Velcro attachment allowed for a better fit and greater adjustability. Ankles, knees, and elbows could be wrapped in seconds, and ice could be applied right where it was needed quickly and effectively.

The orthopedic line with the Body Glove logo got in front of the entire sports world. Soon, other NBA teams were buying the Body Glove orthopedic wraps, and it wasn't long before word spread to other professional sports teams in the National Hockey League, National Football League, Major League Soccer, and Major League Baseball. Players wanted the products, and sales took off.

Magic Johnson was on the cover of *Sports Illustrated* magazine wearing the knee brace, and Body Glove created an entire line of products with his name on them.

Body Glove's orthopedic products catalog cover featuring the Magic Johnson line.
Photo credit: Body Glove International

Billy Meistrell said, "Through our relationship with the Buss family we had the Laker Girls dancing in Body Glove wetsuits and even got a neoprene band put around the basketball pole during a few Clipper games."

Jeanie Buss, executive vice president of business operations for the Los Angeles Lakers, recalls, "Back before the NBA started to regulate advertising activities, we teamed up with Body Glove in several fun ways. Billy Meistrell was a smart marketer and recognized the value of the Body Glove logo. He solved a chronic need for icing injuries and introduced Body Glove to our entire team and its fans."

She added, "After the Laker Girls began to wear Body Glove outfits at games and other events, Body Glove expanded its brand and the Lakers were recognized for teaming up with a cool family-owned company."

One of the offshoots of the neoprene outfits made for the Laker Girls was Body Glove's advance into women's swimwear and related clothing made with neoprene. Bikini and one-piece swimsuits were introduced to active sports markets worldwide. They were

The neoprene wrap around the basketball pole was an innovative marketing technique.
Photo Credit: Body Glove International

Los Angeles Lakers during a photoshoot on Disappearance.
Photo Credit: Body Glove International

followed shortly by neoprene skirts, jackets, dresses, and hats, and even jeans in denim and neoprene combinations.

Little did the Meistrell family know that all of this exposure would lead to a huge number of business opportunities down the road. What they did know, however, was that the second generation had stepped up and was proving that it could and would lead the company into the future. Bill and Bob had accomplished another goal. They had given their children the opportunity to know their fathers, an opportunity Bill and Bob themselves had not been fortunate enough to enjoy.

(Left to right) Bill, Randy, Ronnie, Julie, Billy, Robbie and Bob on the Disappearance.
Photo credit: Body Glove International

17

SURFING GOES PROFESSIONAL

The move to classify surfing as a professional sport began in the mid-1960s. From 1964 to 1968 the International Surfing Federation (ISF) held the World Surfing Championships, and the competition was open to all surfers. However, the ISF wasn't able to create a successful program.

From 1970 to 1975 the Smirnoff World Pro-Am Surfing Championships became the de facto professional contest on a worldwide basis. In 1976, International Professional Surfers (IPS) was created to serve as the governing body of professional surfing, which it did until its demise in 1982.

Original Dive N' Surf team featured in one of the first Surfer magazines. (Left to right) Mike Purpus, Robert August, Rich Chew, Rick Irons Sr. Photo credit: Meistrell Archive

Ian Cairns established the Association of Surfing Professionals (ASP) in 1983. The ASP was able to attract world surfing organizers to its membership, and it became the organization of choice for professional surfers and those seeking to advance to professional status.

Other organizations and contests sprang up around the world to offer amateurs and pros opportunities to win money and recognition, but the purses never reached high figures. What the surfing world needed was corporate sponsors with enough money to make the contests worthwhile and attractive.

Bill and Bob were not really following any of the surfing tours at that time, but they were sponsoring surfers to promote Body Glove's products. They needed top performers on the east and west coasts to support the retailers that were carrying their products. As one of the first companies to do so, Body Glove began sponsoring professional surfers in the late 1960s and into the '70s, and beyond. While there wasn't a corporate team at that time, there were individual surfers, such as Mike Purpus, Rick Irons, Sr., Rich Chew, and Robert August, who received various forms of support from Body Glove. While there may have been some small financial support, most surfers received free Dive N' Surf or Body Glove products and as much promotion as possible through print ads in Surfer magazine.

> Mike Purpus: "I always wanted one of their wetsuits but I couldn't afford it and I just surfed all the time. There was no way I wanted to work for it and they finally asked me to be in an ad in 1968, along with Robert August, Richard Chew, and Ricky Irons. I was all stoked to do an ad and get a free wetsuit. I wore wetsuits every day, no matter what. I wore right through the crotch and butt of that wetsuit!"

In the 1970s, Body Glove added to its team some of the most high-profile surfers in the sport at that time. Gerry Lopez, Jeff Hakman, Rell Sunn, and David Nuuhiwa

First female riders on Team Body Glove. Jericho Poppler (left) invited Rell Sun (right) to join the team.
Photo credit: Body Glove International

added star power to the team. Body Glove worked hard to create team spirit by providing all of its surfers with shirts and gear with the famous Body Glove logo. Bill and Bob were sure that the team spirit would encourage them to hang out with each other at contests and push each other to do well when they were surfing in events together. By doing this, Body Glove met some of the most creative people who were changing the scope of the sport and the lifestyle that went with it. Key among this group of surfers were Jeff Ho, Peter Townend, Ian Cairns, Lewis Graves, and Jericho Poppler.

Known as "The Queen of Makaha," Rell Sun became one of the most popular surfers from Hawaii and a Hawaiian surfing champion.

In 1972, skateboarding had a resurgence when urethane skateboard wheels, called Cadillac Wheels, were developed. They made skateboarding smoother and safer than it had been with the earlier clay wheels, and they allowed riders to perform more adventurous moves at higher speeds. Part of the growth of Body Glove and surfing

Jericho Poppler and Rocky Sabo with the rest of the team.
Photo credit: Body Glove International

Rell Sun sporting the popular Body Glove "Frenchie" wetsuit.
Photo credit: Meistrell Archive

Jeff Ho (right) surfing at the POP Pier in Venice.
Photo credit: Ho Archives

in the 1970s came about through the efforts of surfer and skateboarder Jeff Ho, the owner of Jeff Ho Surfboards and Zephyr Productions.

Jeff Ho, from an area of West Los Angeles near Venice Beach and Santa Monica called "Dogtown," led a group of boys who surfed what was called the Pacific Ocean Park Pier, POP, an abandoned amusement park. It was a dangerous place to surf because of the broken pier pilings and lack of space for all of the surfers who surfed there.

Ho began making surfboards in the middle of Dogtown and soon created a Zephyr surf team of young surfers who had nowhere else to go. They were an aggressive bunch whose boards reflected the influences of Dogtown with designs resembling a graffiti tattoo style.

After surfing, the team took to their skateboards and practiced their new-found surfing moves as they skated the city streets and parks. Using techniques honed on the water, they soon began emulating the classic surfboard techniques of notable surfers, such as Larry Bertlemann, who liked to drag his hand through the wave as he rode it. Ho and his surfers rode their skateboards in the same manner, bending their bodies low to the ground and sliding their hands on the pavement. For this entire team, it was about style; if you did not have it, you were not part of the team!

Jeff Ho: *"Allen Sarlo came to my attention when he was 8 years old. He surfed the Venice Beach Breakwater. I saw him in competitions and surfing at Bay Street in Santa Monica. He had more drive than anyone else and that followed him throughout his entire surfing career. It was amazing to watch him create new moves and push his surfing style to the next level." said Jeff Ho*

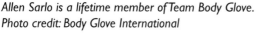

Allen Sarlo is a lifetime member of Team Body Glove.
Photo credit: Body Glove International

Ho and his team wore Body Glove wetsuits while surfing, thereby introducing the brand to a whole new audience. Body Glove brought Jeff Ho onto its team, along with a few of his surfers, including Allen Sarlo and Jay Adams. This expanded Body Glove into the skateboarding world in California and elsewhere. Soon, the Zephyr surfing team, which was also the Zephyr skateboard team, was representing Body Glove in a variety of venues in Santa Monica, Malibu, and coastal California. The famous hand logo sticker turned up in various places as the skateboarders wore it on their clothes and placed it on their skateboards. Ho and his team later became widely popular because of their competition tactics in skateboard events. In 2005, the film *Lords of Dogtown* was released, and movie audiences worldwide learned about these bold trendsetters in both surfing and skateboarding.

Body Glove sponsored the "Bronze Aussies" Ian Cairns (left) and Peter Townend.
Photo credit: Body Glove International

Meanwhile, back on the competition front, professional surfers Peter (PT) Townend and Ian Cairns's company Sports and Media Services started a mini-tour of five events in Southern California, which they called the Grand Prix. PT said, "We convinced Robbie Meistrell to sponsor these five events and they became the Body Glove Grand Prix. Its first year was 1980 and the champion was Bud Llamas." This contest reignited the concept of professional surfing in California. "For Body Glove, this exposure was great and I believe this got Body Glove into the business of sponsoring events," said PT. As a result, Body Glove became more interested in sponsoring professional surfing events as a marketing strategy for the brand.

In the United States, Californian surfer Joey Buran, known as the "Cali-

Joey Buran joined the team in 1984 and went on to win the Pipeline Masters.
Photo credit: Body Glove International

fornia Kid," who had been successful in numerous contests in Hawaii, Brazil, Australia, Japan, and South Africa, including a first place win at the Pipe Masters in Hawaii, launched the Professional Surfing Association of America (PSAA) in 1985. He said recently, "I started the PSAA with the intention to have the best competitive surf tour in the world, thereby giving the American surfers a better shot at being the best competitive surfers on the planet." He wanted to give young surfers opportunities to compete and earn some bucks that he had not had as a young teen. Joey was one of Body Glove's top surf stars at that time.

Joey Buran started surfing at age twelve, in 1973, and became the top-ranked amateur in California at fourteen. At seventeen he turned pro and reached the finals of the Pipeline Masters in Hawaii. In 1980, he became California's first full-time professional surfer and, by finishing first in Brazil, the first Californian to win a world tour event. By 1985 Joey was ranked seventh in the world, the first Californian to make the top ten in the world. He left surfing to enter the ministry in 1987, but later returned and became the head coach of the USA Team. Today, he continues to pursue his love of surfing and his ministerial life in Southern California.

PSAA (Professional Surfing Association of America) created by Joey Buran in 1985.
Photo credit: Body Glove International

In the PSAA's first year, Buran ran its contests at various California locations, including Seaside Reef, north of San Diego. Robbie Meistrell saw how Buran ran the event and how much the surfers liked the contest. Buran suggested that Body Glove take over the PSAA, and Body Glove agreed, buying the PSAA from Buran in late 1985 and hiring him to be the managing director for 1986.

Body Glove reduced the number of contests to eight and raised the purse for each event from $500 to $5,000, thereby attracting more surfers and sponsors.

Body Glove changed the way the contests were run by eliminating the rental of tents, chairs, scaffolding, PA systems, and other equipment in favor of a one-time purchase of everything they needed. This saved the company a ton of money, which it was now able to use to promote surf events and increase the purses.

In the 1987 season, Joey Buran left Body Glove to become a minister, so Body Glove hired Midget Smith, who had worked with Joey, to be the new head judge. The next step was to obtain

Midget Smith later became the head judge of the Bud Surf Tour in 1988.
Photo credit: Body Glove International

Bud Surf Tour logo.
Photo credit: Body Glove International

1987 Bud Surf Tour at Steamer Lane, Santa Cruz, California.
Photo credit: Body Glove International

Bud Surf Tour at Malibu, California.
Photo credit: Body Glove International

a major sponsor, and Body Glove successfully negotiated with Anheuser-Busch, thereby creating the Budweiser US Pro Surfing Tour, known simply as the Bud Pro Surf Tour.

Over the next seven years, the tour reached annual purses close to $500,000, a far cry from the early days before Body Glove's involvement. During this time, the tour's organizers made it a point to travel to both coasts of the United States, where each year at least eight events were held. The location of the contest differed from year to year to maximize the exposure of the tour and its athletes. West Coast sites included San Francisco and all of the Southern California beaches including California Street in Ventura, Malibu, the South Bay, Huntington Beach, Trestles, and Seaside Reef. East Coast events were held at Seventh Street in Atlantic City, New Jersey; Sebastian Inlet in Melbourne, Florida; and Jobos at Isabella, Puerto Rico. The tour also crossed the Pacific to the North Shore of Oahu, Hawaii, for the Pipeline and an annual event at Haleiwa.

After the tour became more successful, Body Glove convinced Don Corsini of Prime Ticket, a regional sports channel covering Greater Los Angeles teams, to televise the Bud Pro Surf Tour events. Through Prime Ticket's national affiliates, such as Sunshine Sports Network in Florida, the pro surfing events were now broadcast to millions across the United States. This public exposure gave both Body Glove and its surfers greater recognition than had previously been achieved. It also made the surfers on the Bud Pro Surf Tour more popular than the ASP because they were on TV in the American market. PT Townend was the broadcast announcer with Bill Macdonald, who later became the Los Angeles Lakers play-by-play television announcer.

The day of a surfing contest, the production crew arrived on the scene, set up broadcast equipment, and interviewed contestants and fans. The recording was aired within a day or two, sometimes even the same day as the event. With the Body Glove-Prime Ticket agreement calling for broadcasts on a regional basis and at least twice nationally, surfing became more popular than ever.

Body Glove also convinced Prime Ticket to give the Surfrider Foundation a thirty-second public service announcement, to promote its ocean protection mission, during every broadcast of a Body Glove surfing contest in the Budweiser Surf Tour. This helped the Surfrider Foundation broaden its membership base, and donations increased substantially.

Although a worldwide pro surf tour existed, Body Glove knew that a small company like itself was not able to sponsor surfers to go all around the world to compete. Also, surfers on the international circuit were out of sight for most of the year and, therefore, not available for photo opportunities and interviews in American markets. Body Glove's direction was to promote American surfers in American venues, thereby promoting Body Glove, an American company. The company saw this as the best way to spread the Body Glove brand while developing an American feeder system of young athletes who could go up the ladder to the pro surfing world tour.

Jeff Booth won the 1988 Body Glove Surfbout.
Photo credit: Body Glove International

1990 Surfbout held at Lower Trestles, San Clemente, California.
Photo credit: Body Glove International

Another Body Glove creation was the Body Glove Surfbout competition, which started in 1988 at a favorite surfing location in Southern California called Salt Creek, off Dana Point. In its second year the event moved to Lower Trestles, just to the south of San Clemente. Known for its incredible surf break, Lower Trestles featured a perfect peak that allowed surfers to go left or right. This offered pro surfers one of the best venues to show off their best possible performance.

In the first Surfbout contest, Jeff Booth won the first place prize of over $30,000, while the 1989 title went to Christian Fletcher. In 1990, at the Lower Trestles, eighteen-year-old Floridian Kelly Slater won the title, his first pro championship title. This win signaled his future career as the most successful surfing champion ever. Interestingly, twenty-two years later, on September 20, 2012, Kelly won his fiftieth title at the Lower Trestles when he took first place at the Hurley Pro, thus becoming the all-time winning professional surfer with eleven ASP world titles.

Kelly Slater won his first professional contest at the 1990 Body Glove Surfbout.
Photo credit: Body Glove International

As surfing continued to grow as a professional sport in the following decades, Body Glove's leadership at the beginning and its support throughout the ensuing years proved to be important decisions for both Body Glove and surfing. Athletes were given opportunities to follow their dreams to become surfing professionals. Careers were created in what had previously been no more than a sport to enjoy when time allowed and the waves cooperated. A whole new industry had been formed, and Body Glove was at its very heart.

Today, decades later, Body Glove is proud of its long commitment to surfing and its diverse product line that allows surfers and others to enjoy the water more comfortably and safely. From its somewhat humble beginnings with the Grand Prix to its current team of professional surfers, Body Glove stands out as the American company most influential in developing professional surfing to the heights it now enjoys.

Body Glove's teams over the years have included these great athletes:

Athletes of the 1960s:
Mike Purpus, Robert August, David Nuuiwaa, Rick Irons, Hobie Alter, Jeff Hakman, Dewey Weber, Richard Chew

Athletes of the 1970s:
Gerry Lopez, Alan Sarlo, Peter Townend, Ian Cairns, Reno Abilara, Larry Bertleman, Nathan Pratt, Rell Sun, Mike Benevedez, Herbie Fletcher, Rocky Sabo, Jay Adams, Jericho Poppler

Athletes of the 1980s:
Rick Waring, Joey Buran, Ted Robinson, Kelly Gibson, Jim Hogan, Brian McNulty, Scott Daley, Charlie Kuhn, Glen Winton, Steve Machin, Dennis Jarvis, Matt Warshaw, David Eggers, Mark Foo, Jeff Booth, Mike Parsons, Kaipo Guerrero, Danny Kim, Scott Waring, Jonathan Paskowitz, Colin Smith, Scott Farnsworth, Michael Lursen

A young Rob Machado smacks the lip.
Photo credit: Body Glove International

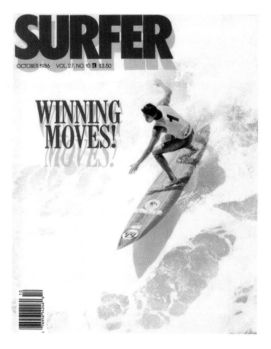

Mark Foo on the cover of Surfer magazine in 1990.
Photo credit: Body Glove International

Athletes of the 1990s:
Pat O'Connell, Vince De La Pena, Rob Machado, Shane Dorian, Matty Liu, Richie Collins, Greg Browning, Kelly Slater, Jeff Booth

Athletes of the 2000s:
Gavin Beschen, Conan Hayes, Bruce Irons, CJ Hobgood, Mike Losness, Holly Beck, Gabe Kling, Tyler Smith

Richie Collins in the air.
Photo credit: Body Glove International

Vince De La Pena in Body Glove black and gold.
Photo credit: Body Glove International

Athletes of the 2010s:
Cheyne Magnusson, Alex Gray, Jamie O'Brien, Anthony Walsh, Matt Pagan, Nate Yeomans

(Left to Right) Team riders Bruce Irons, Gavin Beschen, CJ Hobgood, and Holly Beck.
Photo credit: Body Glove International

(Left to Right) Team riders Jamie O'Brien, Alex Gray, Anthony Walsh and Cheyne Magnusson.
Photo credit: Body Glove International

Body Glove advertisements with team riders from various decades.
Photo credit: Body Glove International

18

PIONEERS OF
THE OCEAN

Bill and Bob's lifetime of ocean exploration, innovative product design, and commitment to ocean protection has been recognized by all major surfing and diving organizations. Starting with the design of a more flexible wetsuit in 1953, everything they did was based on making access to the ocean more comfortable, safe, and fun for divers and surfers. From this central belief came the Body Glove products that now enable people around the world to enjoy all water environments.

The brothers proved that it was possible to build a successful business on a single principle instilled in them at an early age by their mother: treat people fairly, honestly, and with respect. Bill and Bob added to that foundation their commitment to have fun in everything they did. Through their infectious personalities, they influenced those around them to reach farther, do more, and enjoy the process along the way. That was what made Body Glove great through the years, and it is what drives Body Glove today as it enters its seventh decade as a leading example of innovation, creativity, and excellence.

Over their lifetimes…

John M. Olguin Marine Environment Award – On May 20, 2000, the Friends of Cabrillo Marine Aquarium in San Pedro, California, presented Bill and Bob Meistrell the John M. Olguin Marine Environment Award for their lifetime of commitment to protecting and preserving the oceans. Prior and subsequent award recipients include Dr. Sylvia Earle, Jean-Michel Cousteau, Bob Talbot, Wyland, and other notables.

California Wreck Divers' Hall of Fame – In 2001, its first year of existence, Bill and Bob were inducted into the California Wreck Divers' Hall of Fame for their outstanding achievements in the field of ship-wreck exploration.

California Scuba Service Award – Bob was given this award by California Diving News in 1994 "for the invention of a practical wetsuit for SCUBA diving."

Pioneers of Surfing – In 1990, at the Action Sport Retailer Show in San Diego, Bill and Bob, and Jack O'Neill, were recognized as "Surf Pioneers."

Historical Diving Society USA Advisory Board - Bill and Bob served on this advisory board, along with Dr. Sylvia Earle, Jean-Michel Cousteau, Bev Morgan, Scott Carpenter, and other luminaries.

John M. Olguin Award. Photo credit: Body Glove International

California Wreck Divers Award. Photo credit: Body Glove International

Pioneers of Surfing Award. Photo credit: Body Glove International

Bob (left), with Bev and Bill in support roles, at the California Scuba Service Awards gala.
Photo credit: Body Glove International

Bob (left) and Bill with their SIMA
Lifetime Achievement Awards.
Photo credit: Body Glove International

SIMA (Surf Industry Manufacturers Association) Lifetime Achievement Award – Presented to Bill and Bob Meistrell in 2003. SIMA wrote, "Bill and Bob Meistrell, twin brothers, were pioneering watermen and lifeguards whose inventions, talents and exploits helped transform surfing and diving into worldwide phenomena and billion-dollar industries."

Jean-Michel Cousteau and Bob.
Photo credit: Body Glove International

Platinum Pro 5000 Card.
Photo Credit: Scuba Schools International.

Platinum Pro 5000 by Scuba Schools International – From the SSI website: "The SSI Platinum Pro 5000 Diver card is the calling card of the world's most elite water explorers. The list of cardholders is a 'who's who' of diving, containing the world's most prominent dive leaders, scientists, photographers, manufacturers, retailers, and resort operators. Let's put 5,000 dives into perspective. It

| Matt | Jenna | Nick | Bill | Tracy | Bob | Jamie | Makayla | Daley |

Bill and Bob supported by the third generation of Meistrells at the SIMA Lifetime Achievement Awards. Photo credit: Body Glove International

takes 500 dives a year for 10 years, or 100 dives a year for 50 years! That's a lifetime of dedication and commitment to the sport."

In 1993, its first year, the Platinum Pro 5000 Diver card was given to Bill and Bob Meistrell, Dr. Sylvia Earle, Jacques-Yves Cousteau, and Bev Morgan.

The Diving Equipment & Marketing Association (DEMA) Reaching Out Award – The award recognizes "individuals who have made a significant contribution to the sport of diving by 'reaching out' in some special way to improve the sport for everyone." Bill and Bob received the award in 1990.

Bronze Savage Award – Bob and Bill in August 2013 were awarded the "Bronze Savage" award by the Los Angeles County Lifeguard Association. It honors them with admiration and respect for an outstanding career dedicated to public safety.

Both Bill and Bob were the first to admit that any achievements for which they were recognized were really earned by all of the family and employees with whom they worked. They were always ready to place credit on others rather than allowing the focus of any public attention to shine solely on them. While they recognized their individual roles in the company's success, they knew that it takes talented and dedicated people working together to create and maintain the success that Body Glove has achieved. This humble attitude is another major influence from a central person long ago, Bill and Bob's

Bob (left) and Bill with their DEMA Reaching Out award.
Photo credit: Body Glove International

Bronze Savage Awards.
Photo credit: Body Glove International

mother, Mary Elizabeth, who laid the foundation for a life of adventure, commitment, and fun.

Bill and Bob were successful and they were recognized for a variety of reasons, not the least of which was their work ethic and insistence on treating customers with respect and fairness. Coupled with their sense of adventure and their creative minds, the Meistrell twins succeeded where so many others did not.

Bev Morgan believes their success, in part, was based on a simple philosophy: "We just enjoyed what we were doing and kept at it. So that worked out. And they had the right attitude. We wanted to treat our customers fairly and give them a good value for their dollar. And never cheat anybody or anything like that. It just wasn't needed. Just be fair with everybody and things would turn out, and things have turned out."

19

NEW WAVES,
NO OCEANS

n the mid-to-late 1980s, Body Glove realized that only a small portion of the American population participated in surfing and diving, perhaps a total of no more than two million people. Surfing and diving back then usually meant traveling to the west or east coast of the country. While many young people wanted to catch the surfing wave, they simply were left out because they didn't live near an ocean.

Body Glove envisioned a much broader market, one composed of every river, lake, and reservoir across America. Quickly, Body Glove steered a large part of its marketing energy into the freshwater venues where tens of millions of people lived and played. The company figured that the potential for Body Glove products was immense, if only it could transfer its saltwater surfing and diving legacy to freshwater.

Body Glove began an aggressive campaign to introduce its wide product line, plus some new products made just for freshwater, to the vast inland waterways. Water skis, wakeboards, kneeboards, floats, towables, and even soft surfboards, skimboards, and bodyboards were introduced. Of course, all of the company's associated products, such as wetsuits, personal floatation devices, men's boardshorts, women's swimwear and clothing, footwear, hats, towels, watches, and accessories, also were promoted through advertising campaigns and the now famous use of Body Glove professional teams.

By the early 1990s, the company had created teams for water ski, personal watercraft (PWC, also known generally as jetski), and wakeboard competitions. Both its men's and women's teams won championships, with some riders even becoming world champions.

PWC racing was the precursor to the X Games, the wildly successful invention of sports network ESPN, which brought together action sports such as snowboarding, skiing, skateboarding, and surfing, and a host of others called *extreme sports* for their inherent danger. Before the X Games, PWC racing was the most exciting radical sport across the USA. Because a coastline was not needed, it reached across the entire country and brought the extreme sport lifestyle to lakes and rivers.

Body Glove team rider Rob Flores said, "Jet skiing was the original extreme sport even before motocross. It had water, bikinis, and motors—what more could you want?" Event crews rolled into diverse cities and venues, including Austin, Texas, and Lake Michigan. At the time, there were a few supporting sponsors, such as Sea-Doo and Yamaha.

The need for personal gear fueled this sports segment. Body Glove built the most protective suit on the market at the time, which included impact foam on the shins and ankles. Body Glove signs were everywhere on the beach as

Body Glove's Pro PWC racing team.
Photo credit: Body Glove International

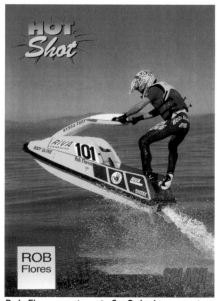

Rob Flores getting air for Splash magazine.
Photo credit: Splash magazine

Disappearance *acted as a buoy for a Long Beach PWC race*
sponsored by Body Glove.
Photo credit: Body Glove International

umbrellas, tents, clothing, gear, and even the grandstands bore the distinctive hand label.

The first personal water craft (PWC) were the stand ups, which were ridden while standing and holding the handlebars. Then sit downs came into the industry, and eventually there was a freestyle division in the contests for cool tricks and stunts, which pushed the limit of what a PWC could do.

Body Glove developed a very diverse team of PWC riders. Rob Flores, Tim Judge, Lloyd Berlew, Matt Alligood, and Dustin Farthing were all National Champions, World Champions, or both. Today, Rob Flores remains the National and World Champion in the USA and Canada.

Body Glove's premiere water-skier in the 1990s was Carl Roberge. Carl won more than one hundred professional victories and twenty-one US Open titles, and was an eight-time Masters Champion in slalom, jumping, and overall. Rhoni Barton was the first female team member and she went on to win numerous water-skiing awards. Freddy Krueger, professional water-skier and team member since the early 1990s, is still on the Body Glove team. He is a Master, World, and National champion known for his jumps. He still holds the world record for highest ski jump (247 feet).

It wasn't long before water-skiing morphed into "ski-boarding" which led to the present day wakeboarding. Body Glove had its finger on the pulse, and when wakeboarding took off, Body Glove was already sponsoring team riders such as Charley Patterson, a pioneer of the sport; Darin Shapiro, a twelve-time World Champion, and Jeff McKee, a team rider known for his amazing style who is still on the team. Today, Body Glove's wakeboard team is one of the best in the world, with National and World champions Rusty Malinoski and Harley Clifford together with a strong list of professional riders including Bob Soven, Trever Maur, Josh Twelker and Melissa Marquardt.

This race suit known as the "swamp cooler" offered superb protection and its perforated neoprene allowed air to penetrate through to chill the water and keep the racers cool. Photo credit: Body Glove International

Lloyd Berloo on cover of Splash magazine.
Photo credit: Body Glove International

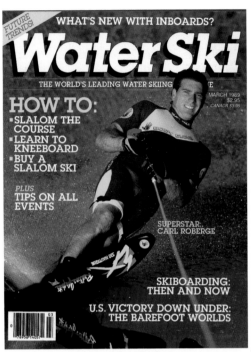

Carl Roberge on the cover of Waterski magazine.
Photo credit: Water Ski Magazine

Harley Clifford, wakeboarding National and World Champion: "Every time I'm with the team and the people who run the company, it's just like being with a family. Body Glove is a company that is dedicated and in love with what they do. All their wetsuits, life jackets, and other gear have so much effort, technology, and passion put into them, and that's why they are the best water sports company there is."

Powerhouse Rusty Malinoski behind the boat in a Body Glove video shoot wearing his team vest.
Photo credit: Meistrell Archive

The sports of waterskiing, PWC racing, and wakeboarding, plus Body Glove's concern for its team riders, are why the advancement of Body Glove's neoprene PFD (personal flotation device) line developed so quickly. The company worked hard to provide greater comfort and safety to its teams and extreme sports enthusiasts everywhere.

Body Glove designed an innovative lightweight, snug-fitting, vest-type PFD that provided greater mobility for the wearer, an important feature for the active movements of these water sports. In time, to meet new demands, Body Glove made neoprene PFDs which also met US Coast Guard standards.

Team rider Harley Clifford getting air behind the boat.
Photo credit: Body Glove International

Another innovation from Body Glove came about because Billy Meistrell had
wanted to help develop the sport of wake surfing, or "freeboarding," since 1985. Wake
surfing is where a person on a surfboard rides the wave created by a speeding boat. The
rider stays close to the stern of the boat, which keeps him in contact with those on the
boat. By positioning himself just right, the wake surfer can get a long ride and a superb
workout. Unlike regular surfing, there is no paddling through surf or being crashed
into shallow water and the ever-present bottom sand. Little did Billy know that almost
thirty years later wake surfing would turn into a national sport with events and championships. Even boat manufacturers are now going after the wake surfing market, with

The Body Glove/ Centurion wake surf boat in Parker, Arizona.
Photo credit: Body Glove International

many adding skid plates and ballast tanks to their boats to displace the water and make the wake bigger for the surfers. Wake surfing allows people everywhere to become surfers, even if there is no ocean within miles.

Just as wake surfing was important in introducing freshwater enthusiasts to surfing, so, today, are wave pools. Body Glove, working with American Wave Machines, has a goal to have a surf center in every big city around the world. Body Glove wants to spread the surfing experience to everybody, and the only way to do that is to bring surfing to them. It is not always easy for people to get to an ocean, so there need to be alternative ways for people to experience surfing. Wave pools are an excellent way to

Mike Lambresi, Oceanside, California
1987 U.S. Surfing Champion

Surfing Champion Mike Lambresi riding a wave pool in the late 80s.
Photo credit: Body Glove International

introduce surfing to those who live far from the beach or who just want to get a feel for what it is like to ride a wave before they venture out onto the ocean.

The same concept applies to Body Glove's sponsorship of cable wake parks. These unique parks provide an overhead cable towing system that pulls wakeboarders around a designated area in water areas, such as lakes or large ponds, without the need for a boat. Not everyone can afford a boat, and a cable park is a great way to introduce people to wakeboarding or to get wakeboarders on the water more often.

Team Rider Cheyne Magnusson riding a Body Glove wave pool in Peru.
Photo credit: Body Glove International

More recently, stand up paddling has taken off as a popular sport. Though people do paddleboard on the ocean, and even ride paddleboards on waves, stand up paddling is a great way for people to explore inland waterways. In lakes and rivers where you used to need a boat or kayak, you can now cruise around and explore while standing up. Body Glove has a full line of stand up paddleboards to keep everyone exploring more and enjoying a wide variety of water adventures.

From a single idea—to introduce the enjoyment of ocean water sports to freshwater venues—Body Glove developed an entirely new industry and set out to provide the best products for this new market. Using innovative designs and styles, it brought surfing, wake surfing, wakeboarding and stand up paddleboarding to millions of people across the United States and worldwide. Its teams and its sponsorships of various contests put Body Glove front and center in these rapidly expanding sports as they introduced new and dynamic ways to enjoy inland waterways.

20

MIRROR TWINS

Bill and Bob were what are called "mirror twins," twins who are a mirror image of one another. If a single fertilized egg splits more than a week after conception, the resulting identical twins can develop reverse asymmetric features. One twin may be right-handed while the other is left-handed, their hair swirls may go in opposite directions, and so on. About 25 percent of identical twins are mirror twins.

In Bill and Bob's case, Bill was right-handed and Bob was left-handed at birth, but the nuns at their Catholic school in Boonville "corrected" Bob to be right-handed. Among other differences, Bill favored the right side of a bed and Bob the left. Also, Bob had an eyetooth on the left side and Bill had an eyetooth on the right side, and in most photos Bob is on the right and Bill is on the left.

Bill and Bob at the helm of Body Glove boat

Bill (left) and Bob on Disappearance.
Photo credit: Body Glove International

Being twins was great fun for Bill and Bob. Not only did they always have each other around as kids, but they had an uncanny way of showing up just when the other needed help. Bob told about one time when he woke up at three in the morning and felt he had to go to Dive N' Surf but couldn't figure out why. He just knew he had to go there. When Bob arrived, Bill was in the shop trying to fix the compressor and he couldn't do it without help. He told Bob, "I was just hoping you'd show up."

Bob (left) and Bill after filling their wetsuits with water at the dive shop.
Photo credit: Meistrell Archive

In school they played some of the same tricks most twins did, such as taking each other's tests and signing in or out for the other. When Bob's son Robbie was small, he sometimes couldn't tell the difference between his dad and his uncle. When he'd ask for a quarter for the gumball machine, Bob would pretend he was Bill and say, "Go ask your dad," and Bill would say "I'm not your dad, he's your dad." Eventually, Robbie figured it out.

Bob (left) and Bill in front of Body Glove International headquarters in the 80s.
Photo credit: Body Glove International

Always jokesters, Bill (left) and Bob liked to play tricks on people.
Photo credit: Meistrell Archive

Bob (left) and Bill among their Body Glove surfboards.
Photo credit: Body Glove International

Scott Daley, former pro surfer and now vice president of marketing for Body Glove, laughingly admits that he solved the problem of not knowing which twin he was talking with by just calling him "Mr. Meistrell."

Observant family and friends had a clue as to which was which by the clothing they wore. Bill always wore long pants and Bob always wore shorts, regardless of the outside temperature.

Bob took great fun in kidding Bill once a year on his birthday. Because Bill was born on July 30 and Bob was born on July 31 (though only twenty minutes apart), Bob teased his brother each year on Bill's birthday by saying he was a year older than Bob.

The "twin story" that really shows their closeness and sense of humor is the one where Bob picked up Bill and they were driving through Redondo Beach on their way to an appointment. Bill had been suffering from Parkinson's, and Bob was concerned about him.

When Bill turned to Bob and asked, "Who are you?" Bob replied, "I'm your twin brother." Bill answered that he didn't have a twin brother. He said he didn't even have a brother. Bob stopped the car, turned the rearview mirror toward Bill, and then leaned over so Bill could see both their faces in the mirror. "See?" Bob said. "Of course you do. Look at us. We're the same."

One more time, Bill said he didn't have a brother, let alone a twin brother. And just as Bob was about to get totally frustrated, Bill smiled and started to laugh.

Bob (left) and Bill on the back of Disappearance *after a dive.*
Photo credit: Meistrell Archive

21

TOGETHER AGAIN

Prior to Bill's death on July 26, 2006, Bill and Bob had never been apart except when they were in the Army for two years in 1950. On June 16, 2013, Bob suffered a heart attack and passed away. Now, they are together again.

Bill spent over sixty years of his life swimming, surfing, and diving in the Pacific Ocean. His passion for the oceans knew no bounds, and he lived and worked tirelessly to create innovative products that would help others to be warmer, more comfortable, and safer as they enjoyed the oceans and water everywhere.

As the more technically minded of the twin brothers, he chose to work mostly in the manufacturing side of the business. The first commercially practical wetsuits he designed and built in the Dive N' Surf shop in Redondo Beach during the early 1950s forged the way for thousands of people to enjoy the cold Pacific waters. Divers and surfers loved the flexible wetsuits Bill made for them.

Bill was a decorated Korean War hero, an incredible man who loved his family, cared about the ocean, gave back to his community, and enjoyed every day of "work."

In a moving remembrance of Bill on October 1, 2006, Body Glove and the Meistrell family invited all surfers, divers, and boaters to join in a traditional waterman formation to move out to the Disappearance, Body Glove's dive boat anchored off Esplanade and Avenue C in Redondo Beach. About three hundred people on surfboards,

Family and friends gathered during the memorial paddle out for Bill.
Photo credit: Body Glove International

paddleboards, and kayaks, as well as others on boats, assembled around a large floating floral display of the black-and-yellow Body Glove logo, which carried Bill's ashes. The night before the memorial, a few long-time employees stayed up until midnight putting together the 6-foot-wide logo made of three thousand black and yellow carnations and one thousand yellow roses. There were about 1,500 people at the memorial reception where Bill's favorite Carl's Jr. spicy chicken sandwich was served.

Bill's brother Bob, son Billy, daughter Julie, granddaughter Jenna, and grandsons Daley, Jake, and Jared, outfitted in their Body Glove wetsuits, got into the ocean with other family members and friends to help the lapping waves open the floral arrangement and gently release Bill's ashes into the ocean he so loved. Lifeguard, Fire, Police,

Military personnel folding the American flag for Billy and Bob.
Photo credit: Body Glove International

Baywatch and Coast Guard boats were all out there and sprayed their hoses in honor of Bill. As the five boats departed, one peeled off, creating the missing-man formation. Military personnel performed a Three-Volley Salute and presented the family with a folded American flag.

After Bill's passing, Bob remained the single visible link to Body Glove's past. He appeared at the headquarters offices daily and spent time with everyone, sharing his unique blend of humor and encouragement. Accompanied by Patty, he actively joined discussions about new products and markets, and often reminded everyone to keep their focus on the company's history while moving forward into new adventures.

Bob's contributions to diving and surfing are legion. Bob continued to give back to his community right up until his death. He took groups out on Disappearance at least twice a week for trips they had bought through donations to one charity or another.

The impact of Bill and Bob's loss has not fully settled on the company. While their absence is felt every day in the office, especially by family members, what keeps everyone going are the memories of Bill and Bob, who will never be far away.

Bill and Bob loved diving at Catalina Island, especially around Ship Rock, off the northeast coast. It was the twins' favorite dive site. Their favorite dive of all time was when they took their dive gear and scooters (underwater propulsion devices) and

The Meistrell family around the Body Glove logo of roses spreading Bill's ashes.
Photo credit: Body Glove International

set out to explore the area. They roamed around Ship Rock and went off in one direction and then another where they saw garibaldi, sea bass, and barracuda in depths ranging from 10 to 135 feet. When they were gone longer than expected, the family worried about them and thought they'd

Paddlers splashing the ocean in honor of Bill.
Photo credit: Body Glove International

either been swept out to sea or drowned in some deep cavern.

Ecstatic over their underwater fun, and laughing wildly, Bill and Bob showed up just before family members alerted Baywatch. They had so much fun together that they had forgotten about time and other people. Ship Rock was their special place to dive, and the twins were in their element.

Lifeguard, Fire, Police, Baywatch and Coast Guard boats salute Bill with one peeling off to signal "man down."
Photo credit: Body Glove International

Bob steering his yellow dinghy on a jaunt away from Disappearance.
Photo credit: Body Glove International

Perhaps it was only fitting that Ship Rock was where Bob would end his days on the ocean. He and Patty had taken the *Disappearance* to Catalina Island for the Father's Day weekend in preparation for the twenty-two-mile Rock 2 Rock paddleboard race from the island to San Pedro, California, that Sunday.

Bob's great-nephew Daley was competing, and the Disappearance was to be the lead boat for the race. For the first time ever, the boat's twin engines failed, and Bob went into the engine room to find and fix the problem. Shortly, others on the boat discovered that Bob had died while below. Despite heroic efforts by family, friends, and Baywatch lifeguards for over two hours, Bob did not survive.

At the time of this printing, Bob's memorial service, a traditional waterman's paddle out, is scheduled for 9:00 AM on September 15, 2013 at the south side of the Redondo Beach Pier. Those who knew Bob are invited to join the Meistrell family on surfboards, standups, kayaks, and boats for the memorial service at the *Disappearance* anchored just offshore. Bob's three sons Robbie, Ronnie and Randy, and their families, will be joined by Bob's nephew and niece, Billy and Julie, and their families, to gather around a giant flower wreath in the shape of the classic blue and white Dive N' Surf logo. After a message and prayer by a priest, the family will disperse the wreath's flowers to allow Bob's ashes to return to the ocean he so loved. Baywatch, Harbor Patrol, Coast Guard, Police, and Fire boats with crews will be on hand to honor Bob and a military contingent will fold the American flag and present it to Robbie and the family.

Following the memorial, the public is invited to a reception at Redondo's Seaside Lagoon just south of King Harbor. Special events are planned during the reception, which is designed to be a celebration of Bob's life, to allow family and friends to share their favorite "Bob stories."

Bill and Bob are together again.

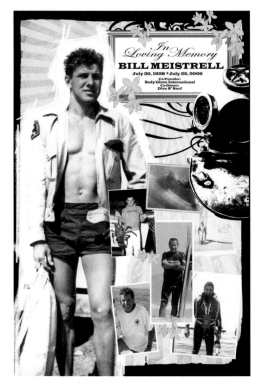
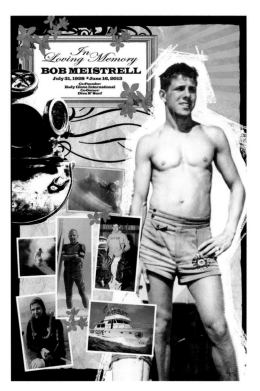

Bill and Bob's memorial posters.
Photo credit: Body Glove International

22

TODAY AND TOMORROW

Body Glove's 60 Year Anniversary logo.
Photo credit: Body Glove International

Today, sixty years after its modest start, Body Glove International is a multi-million-dollar marketing and branding giant in water sports with thousands of products in more than sixty countries. It has international offices in Japan, Thailand, Malaysia, Hong Kong, New Zealand, Australia, Chile, Peru, Brazil, Panama, Canada, France, and Dubai.

Bob Meistrell recounted how he and Bill enjoyed going to work every day and how fortunate they were to meet so many great people over the years. They had an exciting and fun life, which they wouldn't have changed for anything. Beside their three child-hood goals—to own a submarine, to go deep-sea diving, and to hunt for treasure—they also set three other goals for their lives when they started their business. They wanted to live less than five miles from where they worked, make a little money, and have a lot of fun. They knew, too, that they wanted to bring their kids into the business because Bill and Bob didn't experience life with a father and they wanted to make sure their families didn't miss out on the opportunity to be with them as much as possible.

Along the way they maintained their belief that businesses should treat their customers with respect, honesty, and fairness—a code they passed on to everyone who came to work in the company, whether family or not. As a result, sixty years later Dive N' Surf and Body Glove are recognized for their strong business ethics and quality customer care. Bev Morgan, diving legend and early business partner in Dive N' Surf, summed it up well in an interview at his California home in late 2012 when he said, "They worked hard and were honest. That's why they're still in business today."

A good example of this approach to business comes to life in a story Bob loved to tell about a man who came into Dive N' Surf in the early days after it had become a Boston Whaler boat dealer. Bob sold the customer a used boat, two motors, a trailer, life jackets, and an assortment of gear totaling $1,700. When he handed the man the receipt, he told him to bring anything back within thirty days if he wasn't satisfied with it. That was Bill and Bob's policy.

Well, twenty days later, the man showed up with the boat on the trailer and everything looked as if he'd banged it into every dock, jetty, breakwater, buoy, and pier along the California coast. The man said he wanted his money back.

Bob looked at him, looked at the mess before his eyes, and went into the shop. In a few minutes Bob came out and handed the man a check for $1,700. The man was shocked. Bob said, "A deal is a deal."

The man said, "I just wanted to see what you would do. Now that I know how to drive a boat, I want to get a new and better boat." The man handed the check back to Bob and bought $7,500 of goods, including a new boat, motor, and all the accessories.

Body Glove remains one of the only American, family-owned and family-operated businesses in the diving and surfing industry. It hasn't sold out to corporate investors driven by earnings per share, often at the expense of quality and creativity. It hasn't stopped leading the way to new and innovative materials, styles, and products. From

Disappearance *cutting through the Pacific Ocean.*
Photo credit: Body Glove International

its small beginnings in a dive and surf shop so close to the ocean that waves crashed against it, to a new international headquarters built around its iconic Dive N' Surf facility on Broadway, Body Glove continues to embody what Bill and Bob said they always wanted to do: "Love what you do, do what you love," and the rest will happen naturally.

And happen it did. Today, Body Glove enjoys an international reputation for innovation, creativity, honesty, and quality that few other companies can claim. Body Glove continues to manage its growth through strategic planning, astute marketing of its brand, personal management of business relationships, superb customer service, and careful attention to quality.

Body Glove's president, Russ Lesser, said, "Bill and Bob Meistrell created a company based on a dream of life in the water, and this dream continues through the Meistrell family's standards of excellence in product design, respect for the natural world, and deep-rooted values in water sports. We are still owned by the same family that founded the company, and our management team consists of people who have lived, surfed, and dived in the Southern California area all their lives. We are not run by public shareholders, investment bankers, or boards of directors. As a result, we are able to relate and react to the needs and wants of today's water enthusiasts around the world. Our goal is to continue to produce new, innovative, and improved products that help people enjoy their water and other active lifestyle experiences."

As Body Glove prepares for its next adventures, the future looks bright. Its rich history is the foundation on which it continues to build its business, always maintaining its commitment to its customers, partners, and friends. And Body Glove remains committed to protecting the oceans and inland waters for future generations.

"Do what you love, love what you do."

Researching and writing this book was an amazing time in my life. The opportunity to spend time with Bob Meistrell and learn firsthand how twin brothers created a legacy by doing what they loved was a wonderful experience. My visits with Bob and Patty were special times, which I will cherish forever.

While many people helped create this book, I especially want to thank the Meistrell Second Generation, Scott Daley, and Jenna Meistrell, who put their hearts and souls into helping me bring *Fits Like A Glove: The Bill and Bob Meistrell Story* to readers everywhere.

If there are any errors in the book which escaped the editing process, I am solely responsible for them.

Frank Gromling
Flagler Beach, Florida

ABOUT THE AUTHOR

Frank Gromling is an award-winning author of books about nature and conservation. He is a frequent speaker at national conservation and publishing events, including BLUE Ocean Film Festival (Monterey, California), Publishing University (New York, New York), and numerous local and state venues.

His publishing house, Ocean Publishing, has produced twenty-six titles since its creation in 2002, including a series about the National Marine Sanctuaries with noted ocean protector Jean-Michel Cousteau. Ocean Publishing has twice received the prestigious Benjamin Franklin Award, as well as several first and second place awards at the state level.

Frank is active in ocean protection activities, including offshore whale research, and serves on various conservation, business, and government committees. He is an elected commissioner in the oceanside town in Florida where he resides with his wife, Bibi.